Susie Polzin has been doing palmistry for almost forty years and has condensed her findings into this easy-to-read guide so that people may use it as a tool to help themselves and others, and to understand how it may enhance their lives to better their chances at happiness and success.

Susie Polzin

MODERN-DAY PALMISTRY

AUSTIN MACAULEY PUBLISHERS™

LONDON · CAMBRIDGE · NEW YORK · SHARJAH

Ordering Information
Quantity sales: Special discounts are available on quantity purchases by corporations, associations, and others. For details, contact the publisher at the address below.

Publisher's Cataloging-in-Publication data
Polzin, Susie
Modern-Day Palmistry

ISBN 9781641824255 (Paperback)
ISBN 9781641824262 (Hardback)
ISBN 9781645364306 (ePub e-book)

Library of Congress Control Number: 2020925539

www.austinmacauley.com/us

First Published (2021)
Austin Macauley Publishers LLC
40 Wall Street, 33rd Floor, Suite 3302
New York, NY 10005
USA

mail-usa@austinmacauley.com
+1 (646) 5125767

Table of Contents

Introduction

In this book, I have tried to make the subject of palmistry as easy as I can for you to learn. It is a very complex subject but it does get easier the more you do it. It is an exact science, so you can't go wrong. To make things easier to see, you should use some talcum powder and a magnifying glass and a piece of paper for the mess. If you are doing a full reading, it helps to relax the person first. You can do this by either getting the person to give their hands a quick shake or, as I do, hold their hands in yours for about ten to twenty seconds first, to relax them. Just so their fingers are sitting naturally as they are, so you can get a true reading, and always start by asking if they are right or left-handed. Never be shy when you are learning; it is always interesting to see and learn all the different things. I know to this day, as soon as I mention that I do palmistry, the first thing people do is show you their hands and ask about themselves. It certainly makes for interesting conversation.

First Thing Is to Get to Know the Hand by the Common Palmistry Terms

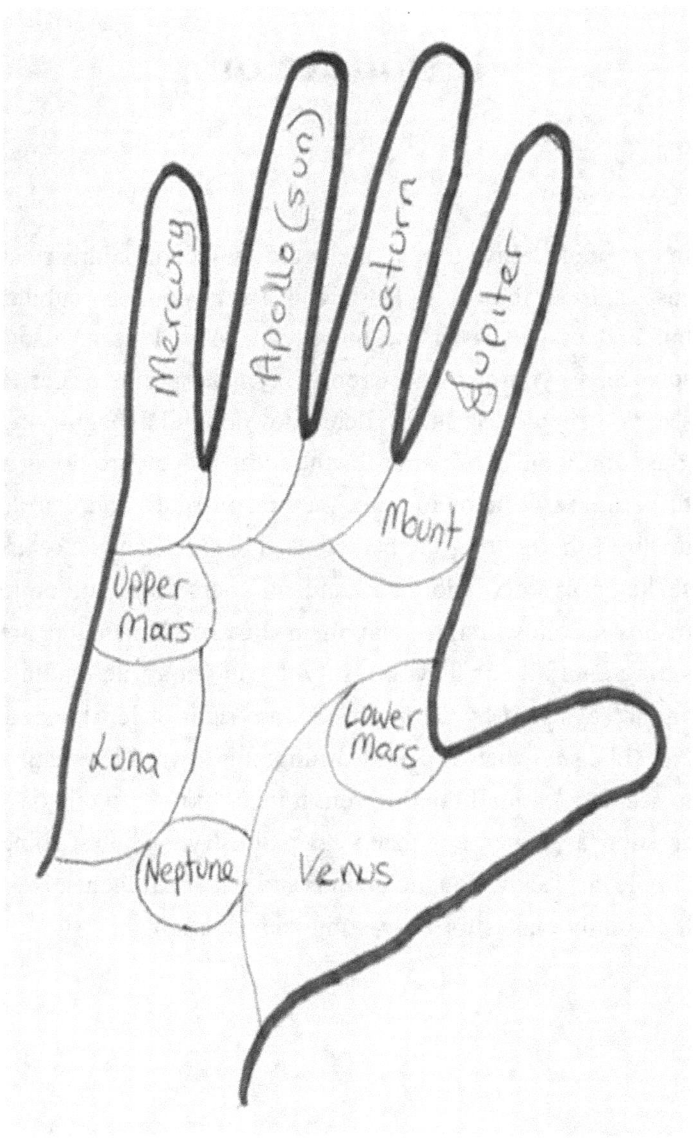

Do We Read Both Hands?

The answer is yes. Ask if they are right or left-handed. Whichever is the hand they write with is usually the dominant hand. Sometimes, you just have to figure it out as you go if the person does not know.

Say the person is right-handed. I would say that the left one is the one they are born with and it never changes and the right hand changes as they grow and change, hence, you must compare them both as you go.

The left hand could also be the person they are on the inside and the right hand is what they like to show the outside world. The opposite would be true for the left-handed person. Sometimes people hold traumatic events on the less dominant hand. You should always study both in a reading.

Also, people don't realize that they can grow and shrink their fingers. They can also straighten them or make them grow crooked, so remember this when you are doing a full reading.

When doing a full reading after getting the person to relax their hands, just ask them to put their hands face down with the palm on the table in front of them. This is when you can ask them if they are right or left-handed, then start with the veins and move on to the positioning of the fingers and the thumb, knotty knuckles, fingertips, etc. The palms and the lines always come last in a full reading.

Chapter 1

Jupiter – The Index Finger

This finger is to do with your personal goals and ambitions in life, also your faith or religion, and includes your self-confidence or self-esteem.

Normal length – is about halfway between the top and second phalange on the middle finger. The person would be confident and capable of standing on their own without the need to lean on other people.

Long – Confident, but if it's too long, can be bossy.

Short – Self-criticism, insecurity, need to lean on others, self-doubt. (This is where you would teach the person how to grow it with self-nurturing techniques instead of beating themselves up with doubt and criticism.)

If the dominant hand has a Jupiter finger that appears heavier set than the passive hand, it means that the person is a lot more self-aware now than they used to be.

If the Jupiter finger is short but also juts out – The person might become loud and aggressive, as well as the above mentioned.

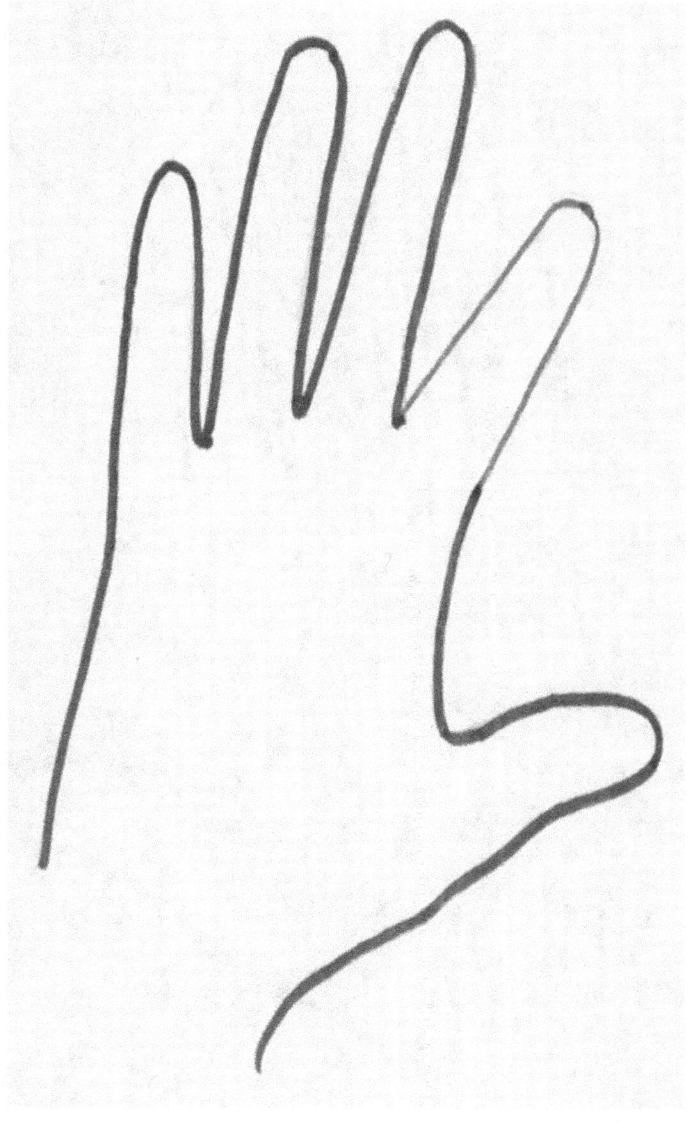

If the Jupiter finger leans in towards the Saturn finger – The person is a collector. When they start to run out of room, the Jupiter finger on the dominant hand will start to straighten.

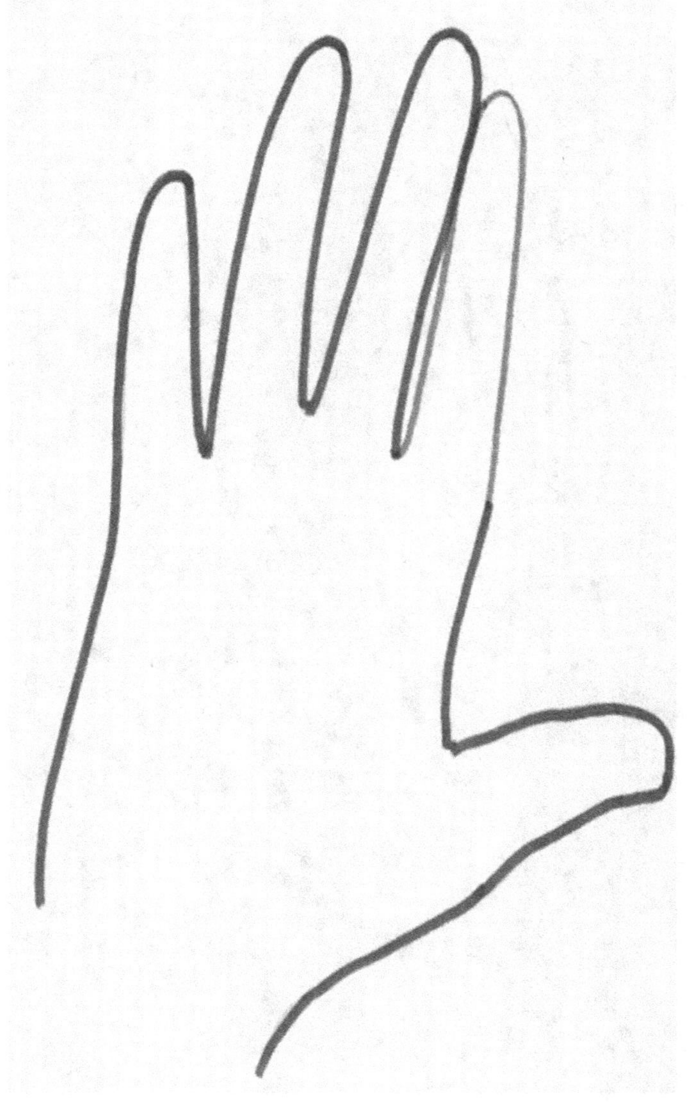

If there is a gap between Jupiter and Saturn – It means that the person is very good with making big decisions, would be handy for a supervisor or in any role that needs to be able to make good decisions.

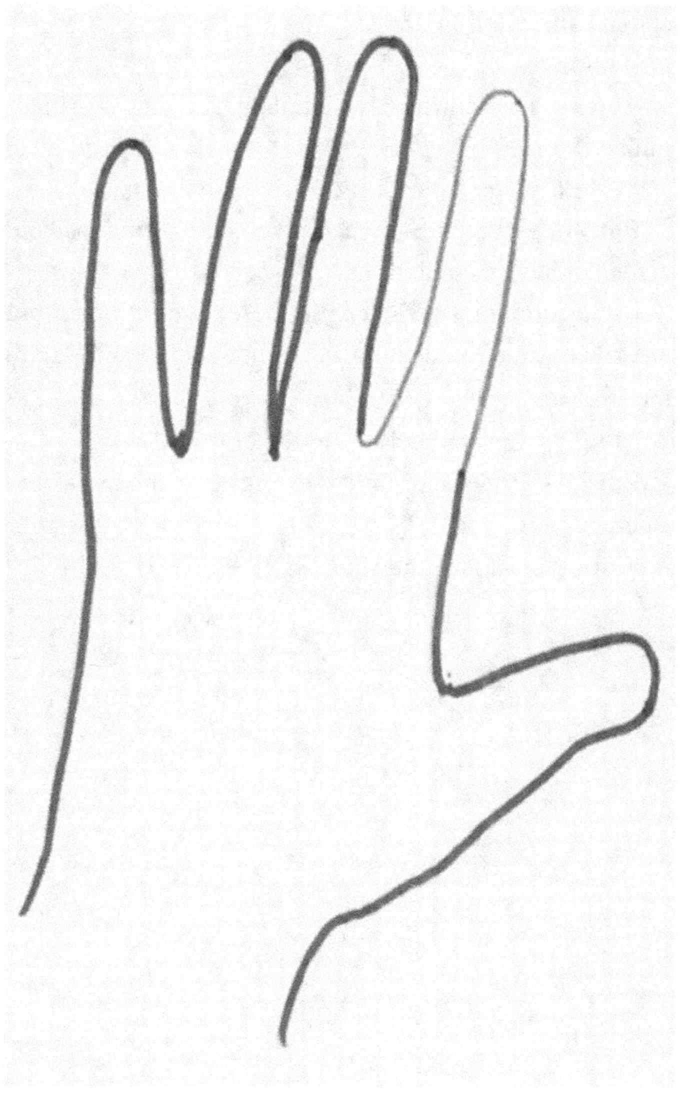

If the Jupiter finger bounces out from the Saturn finger when relaxed – The person doesn't like authority figures or anyone telling them what to do, which also means they are best off working for themselves.

Fingerprints, tips, and nails – Relates to the person's personal ambitions and goals.

Phalanges

Top – Thoughtfulness, intelligence, and spiritually minded if long.

Middle – Business ability. Also, logic.

Bottom – Practical, when it comes to the person's personal goals and ambitions.

If they are not a good length, these descriptions should help to see what is needed to work on. Same goes for all the other fingers.

Mount – Located below the finger.

Large – Pride and ability to organize others, a good leader.

Flat – Self-doubt and shy.

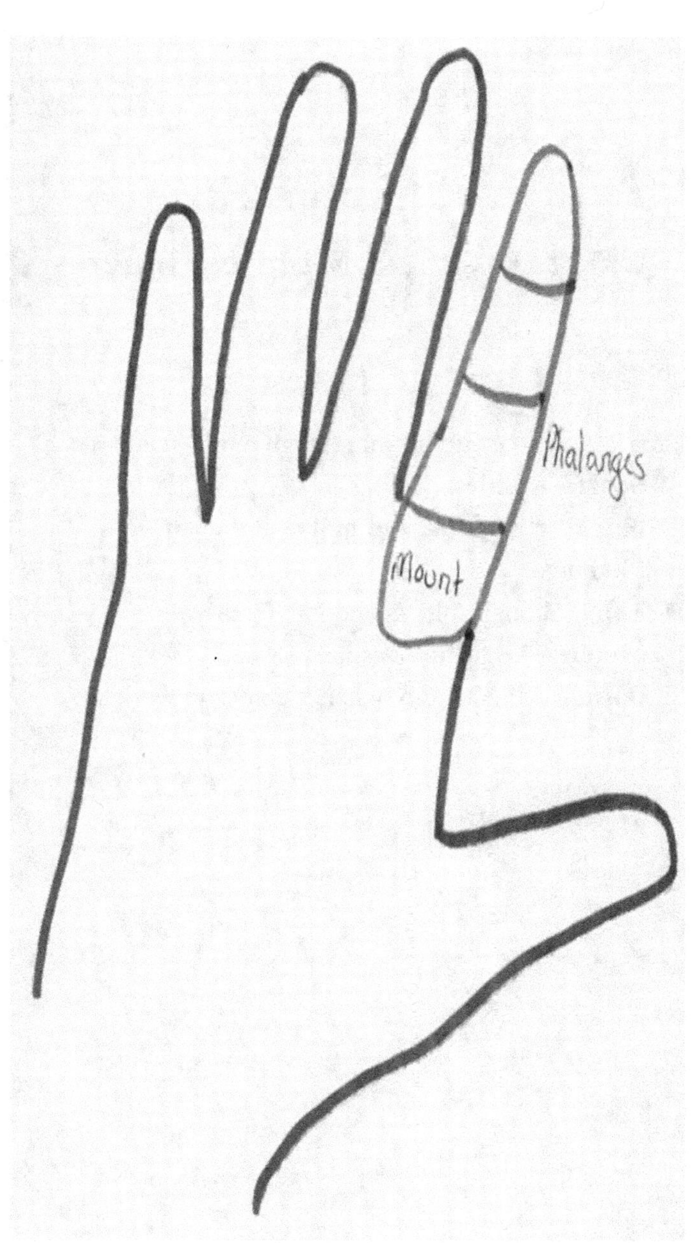

Phalanges
Mount

Chapter 2
Saturn – The Middle Finger

Long – A serious turn of mind, high moral standards.

Short – Reckless.

Fingerprints, tips, and nails – Relate to work.

Phalanges

Top – Thoughtfulness and intelligence.

Middle – Logic and business sense.

Bottom – Practicality when it comes to work.

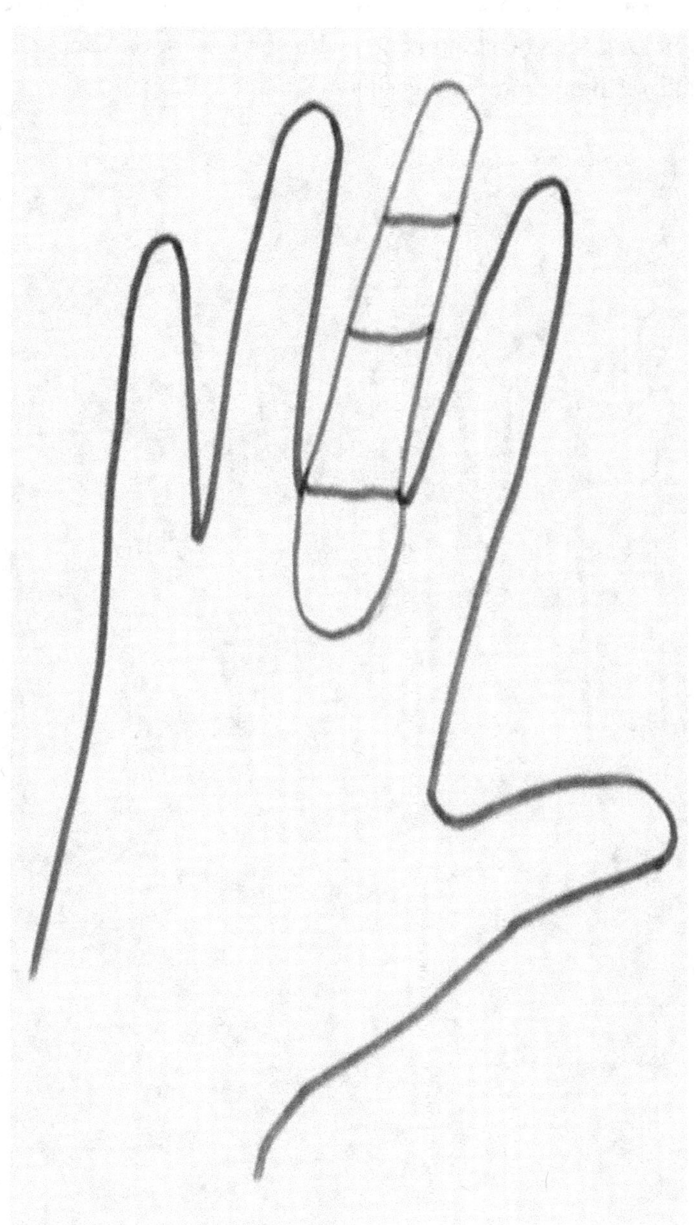

Leaning towards Apollo – Pessimistic or negative thinking (can be straightened with some work on your self-talk). I'll talk more about this in Chapter 19.

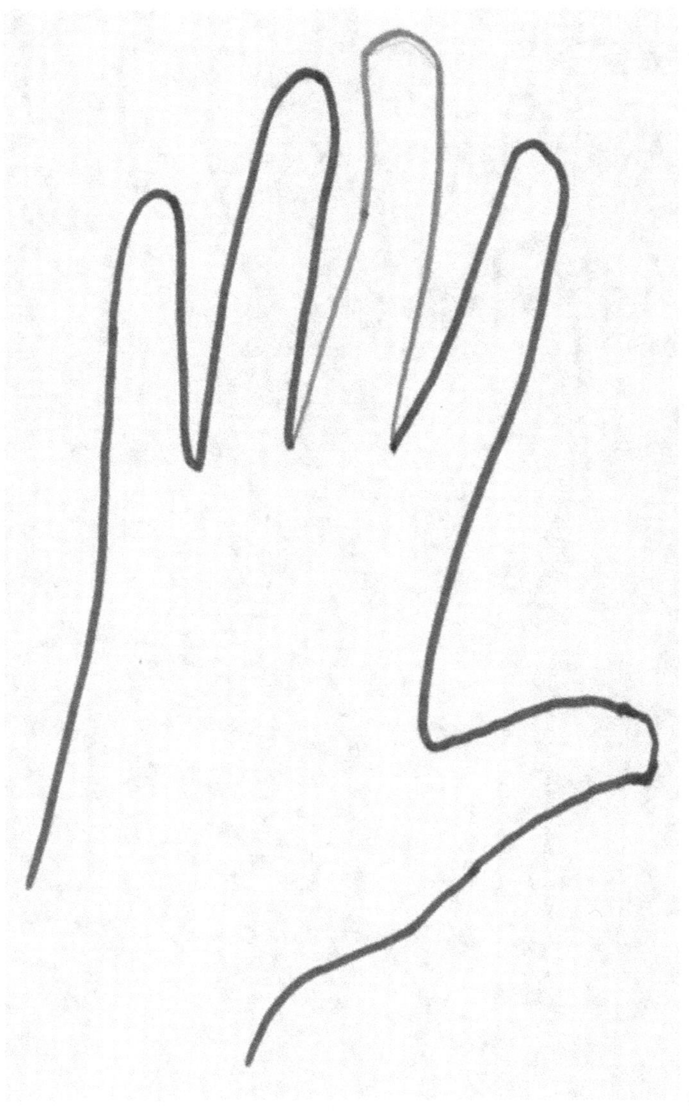

Chapter 3
Apollo – The Ring Finger

Also, the finger of the sun in palmistry terms.

Normal length is halfway up the top phalange of the middle finger.

Long – Creativity.

Fingerprints and tips – Relate to creativity.

Phalanges

Top – Ideas (also, if long compared to other finger tops, it means the person would be good at writing poetry).

Middle – Creative business skill, logic.

Bottom – Practicality in creativity.

Besides creativity, this finger represents the happiness and success a person will achieve in life and the ability to be able to feel it.

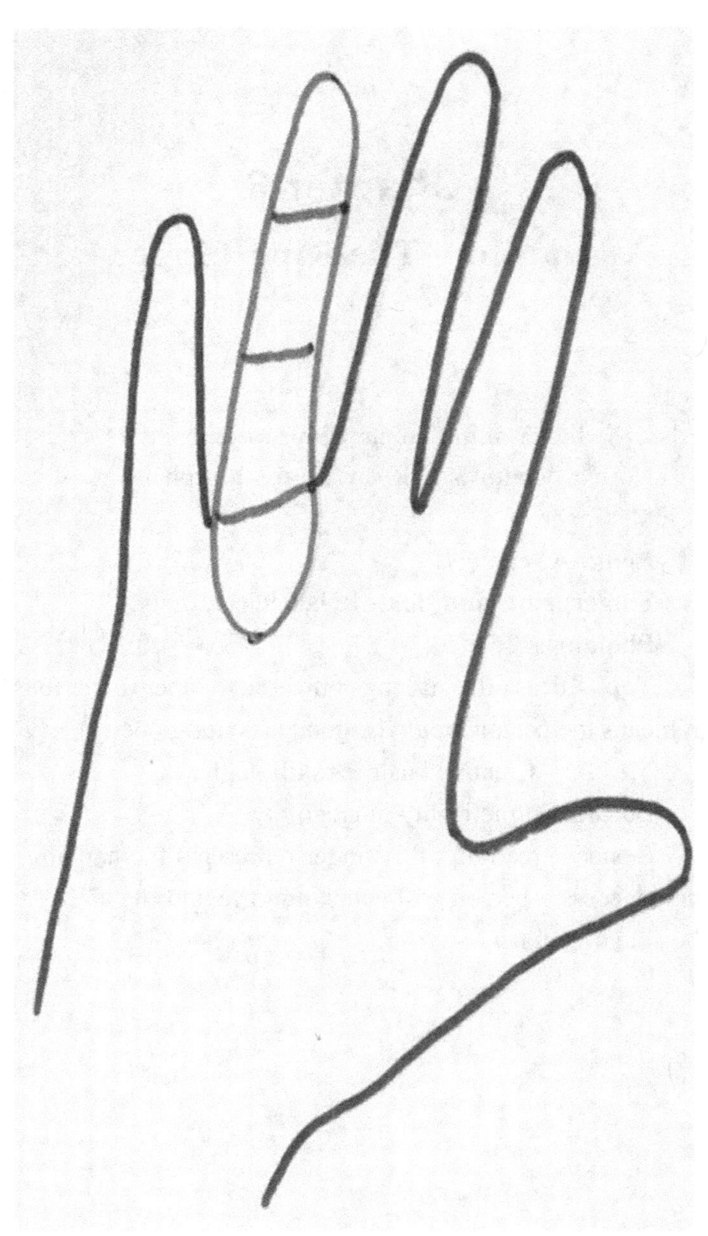

Leaning towards Saturn – Means the person will operate a lot on the feeling of guilt. They feel guilty, so they jump up and do what needs to be done out of the feeling of guilt, but it also means that whatever the person does for a living, they need to get heartfelt satisfaction out of what they do to enjoy it. If not, they will not like it at all.

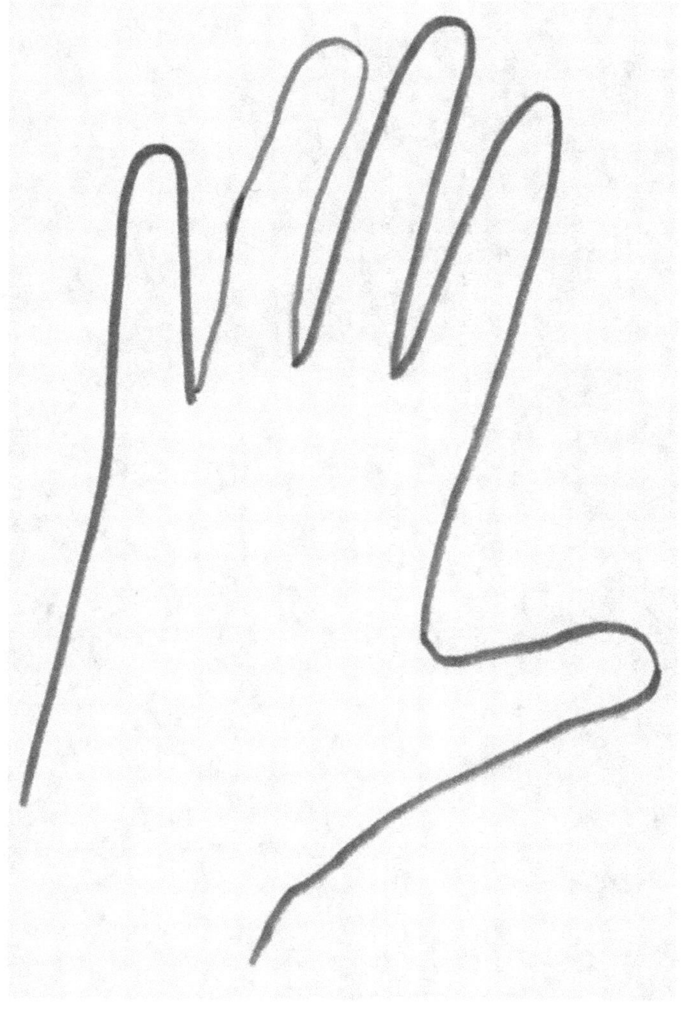

If the Apollo finger stands close beside the Saturn finger – The person is good with a budget; check both hands, could have changed over time.

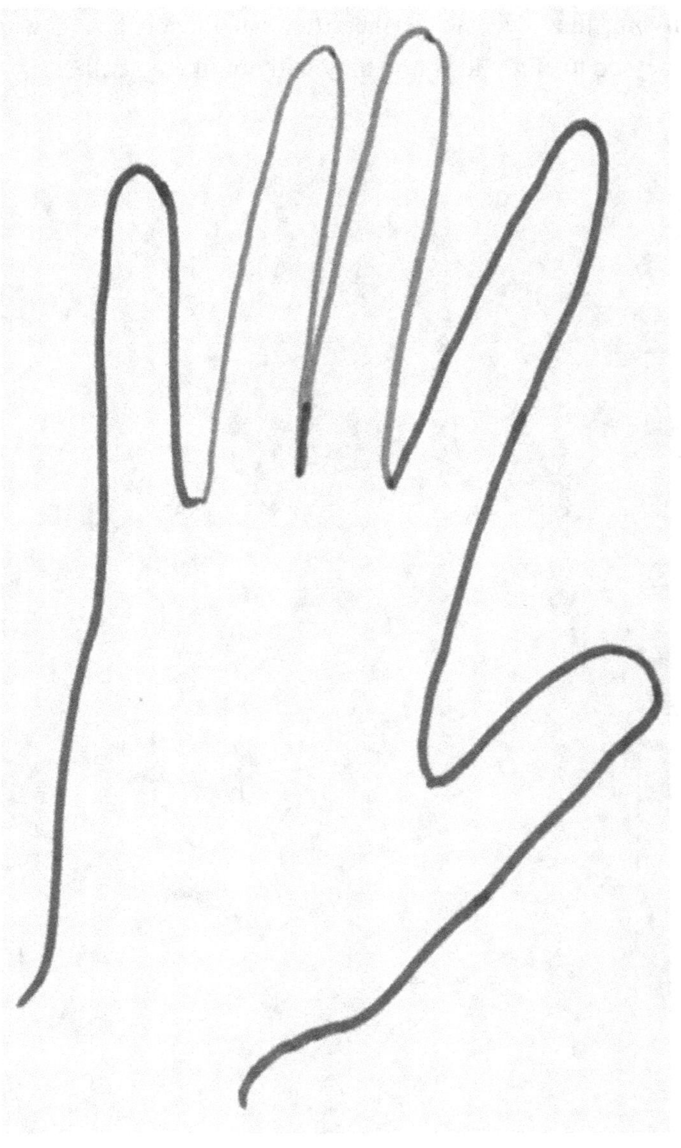

If the Jupiter and Apollo fingers are the same length

– It means the person is a risk-taker.

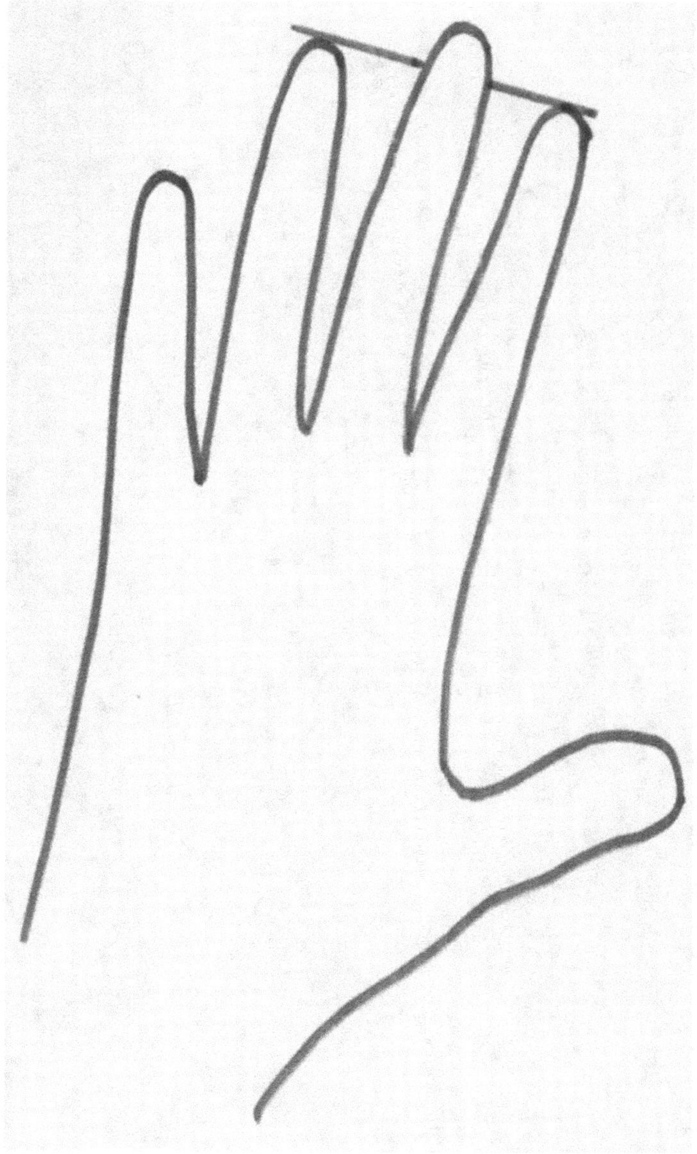

If they are different lengths – They are a cautious person. Check both hands.

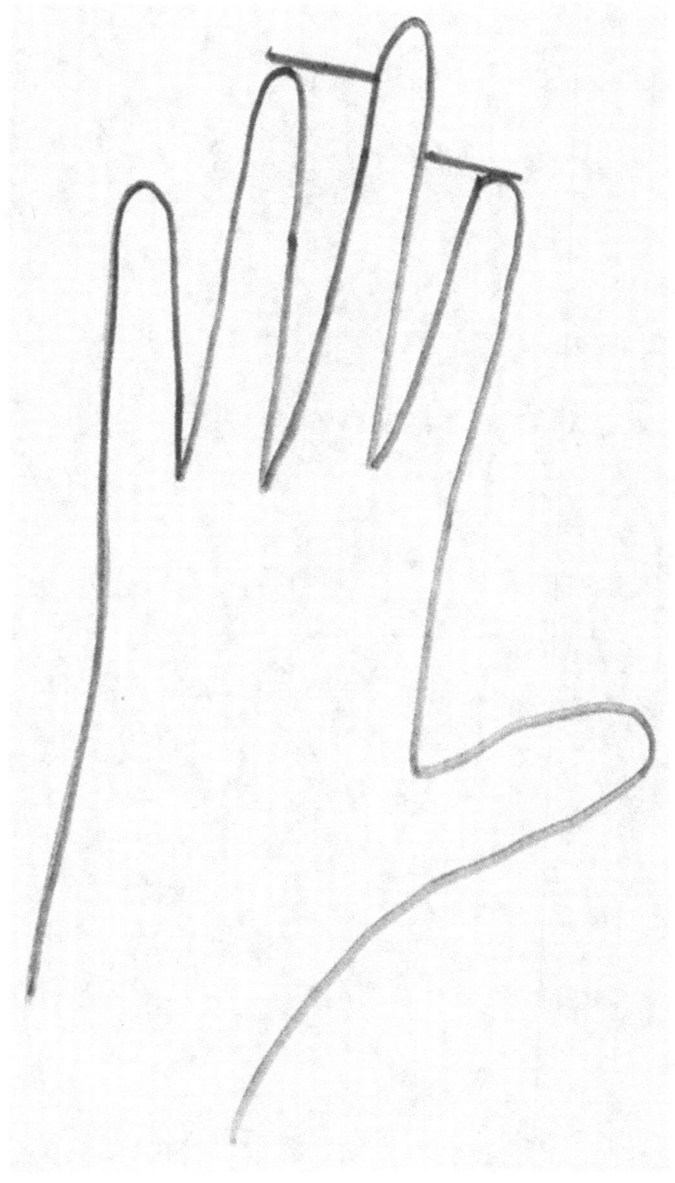

Chapter 4
Mercury – The Little Finger

The Mercury finger has a few different meanings; these things include communication, sex, and a representation of self.

Long – A good communicator: good with public speaking, etc.

Short – Hard for the person to put their thoughts and feelings into words (writing stuff down may help). Also, emotionally immature.

Fingerprints, tips, and nails – Relates to self.

Phalanges

Top – Speaking ability.

Middle – Organizational ability.

Bottom – Practicality, when it comes to yourself in a physical sense, so exercising regularly and looking after yourself physically, as in clothing, food, and shelter.

Sometimes you may see a Mercury finger with four Phalanges. Treat it the same as a long little finger. So they are very good at putting their ideas into words and good with public speaking. Well organized and are practical person when it comes to exercise and looking after themselves.

When you see only two phalanges, it means the same as the small Mercury. As in, emotionally immature.

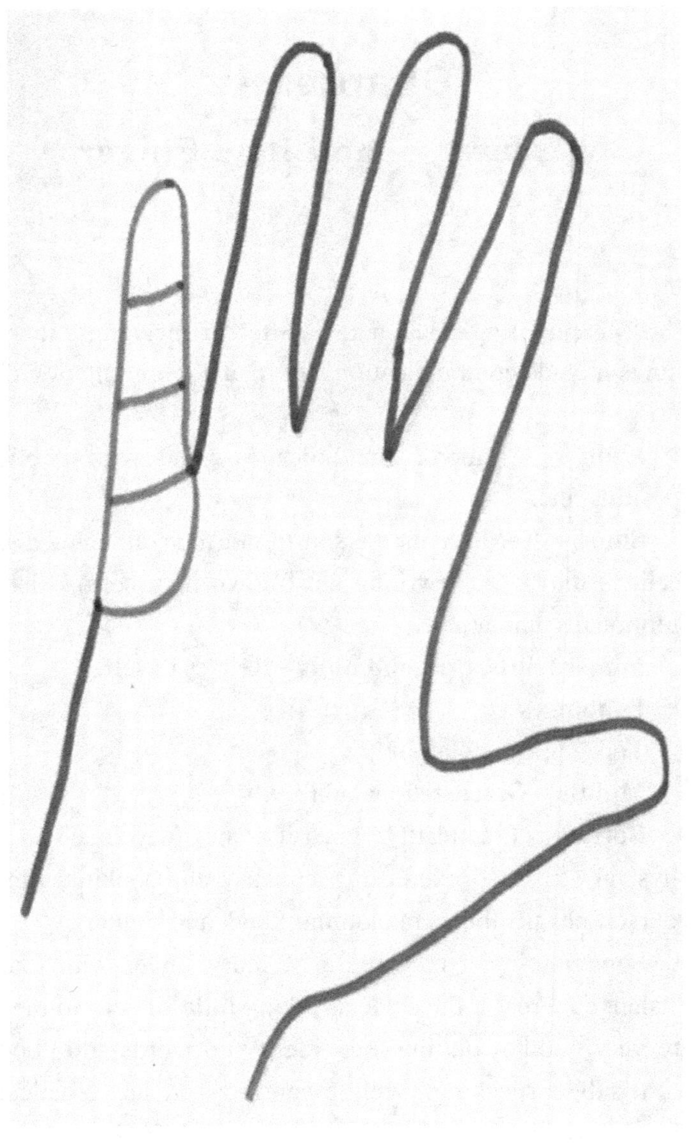

If the top is bulging – The person is full of ideas

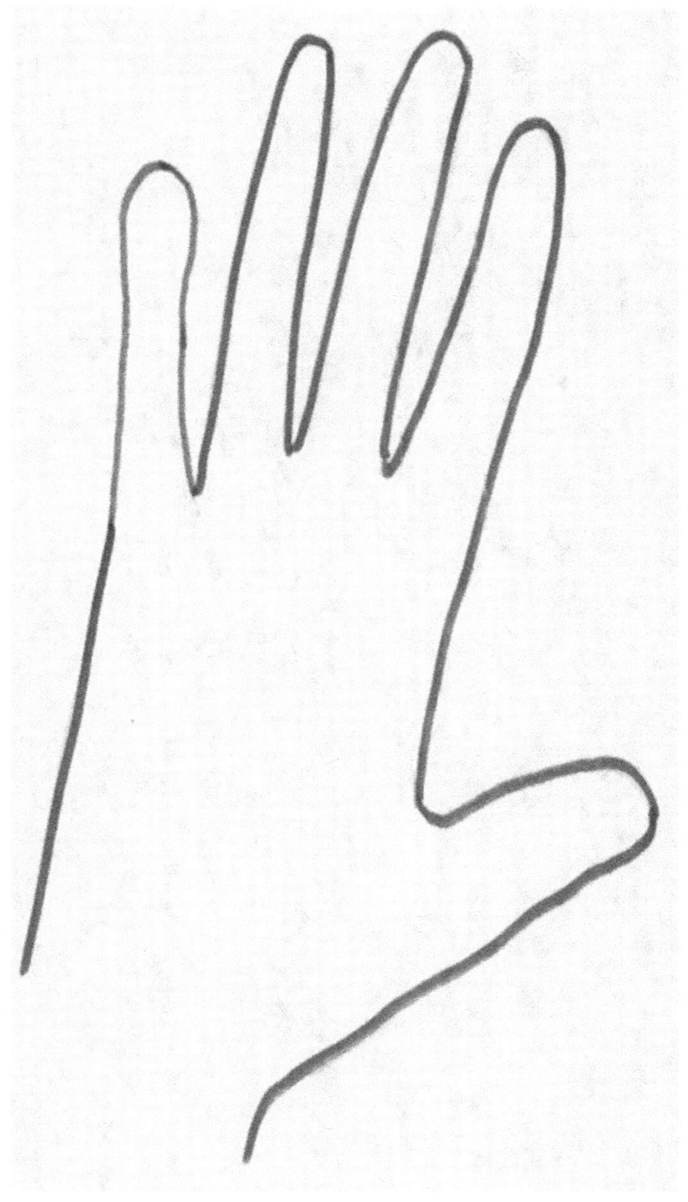

Sitting low on the hand – Something from the person's past is impinging on the present.

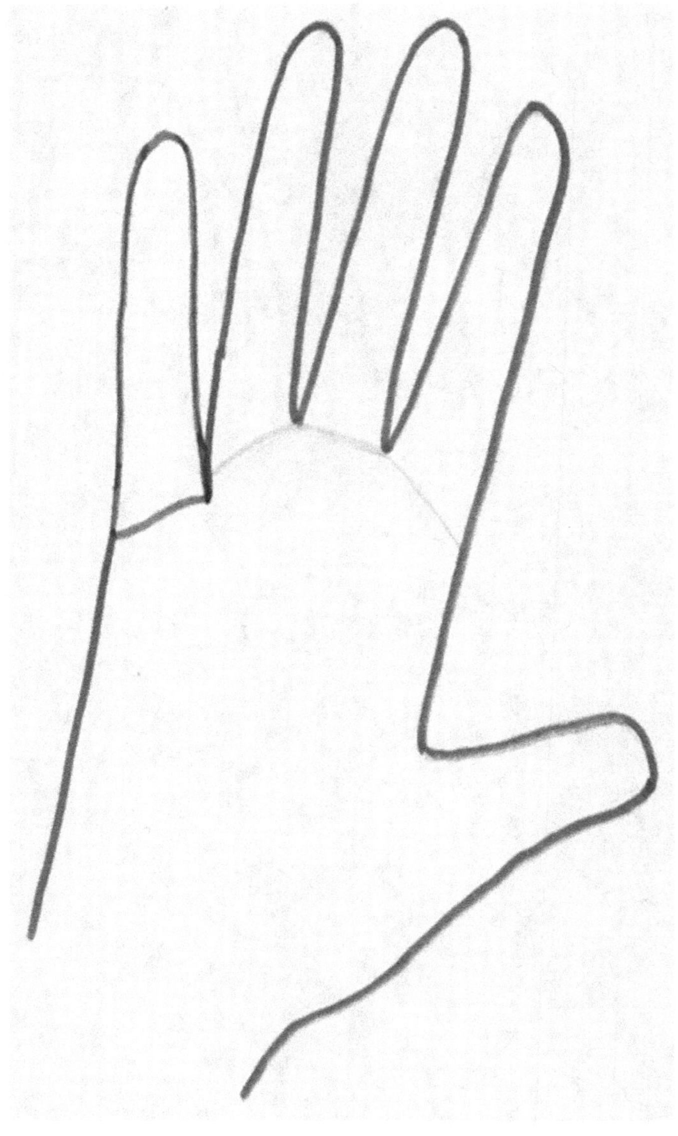

Jutting out – It means at the time of the reading, they are having relationship issues. For example, I was watching the television, and a reporter was interviewing Delta Goodrem and asked her about her relationship with Mark Philippoussis. At the time, she was saying how great everything was but her little finger was jutting out and, needless to say, not long after, they did split up.

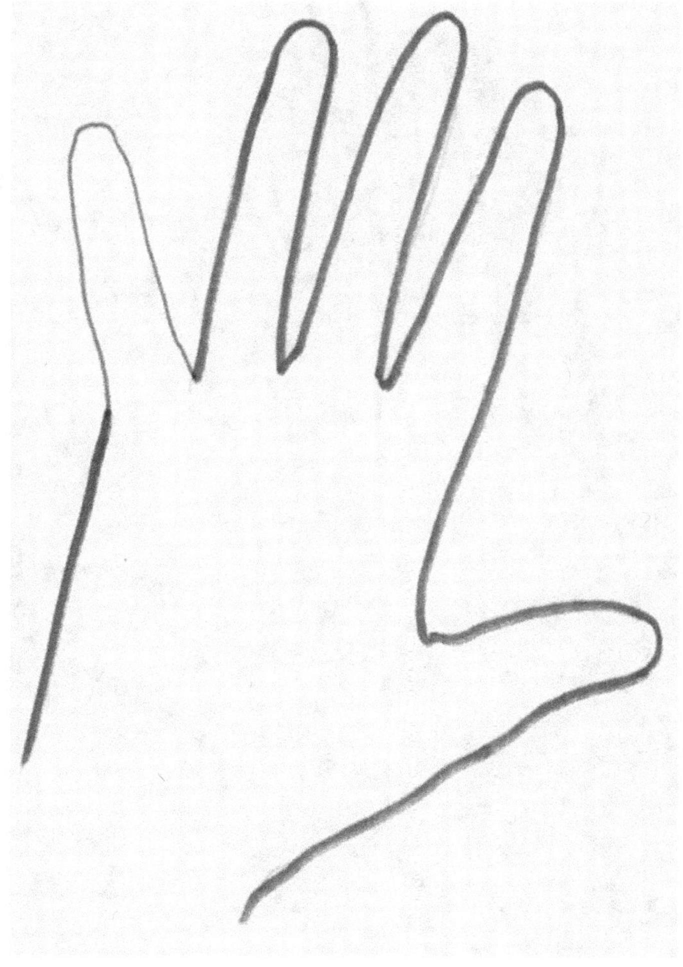

Crooked – A lot of other palmistry books will say that this is the sign of a conman and a liar and rarely it is. What I have found it to mean is, in most cases, the person keeps a certain part of themselves hidden from the outside world.

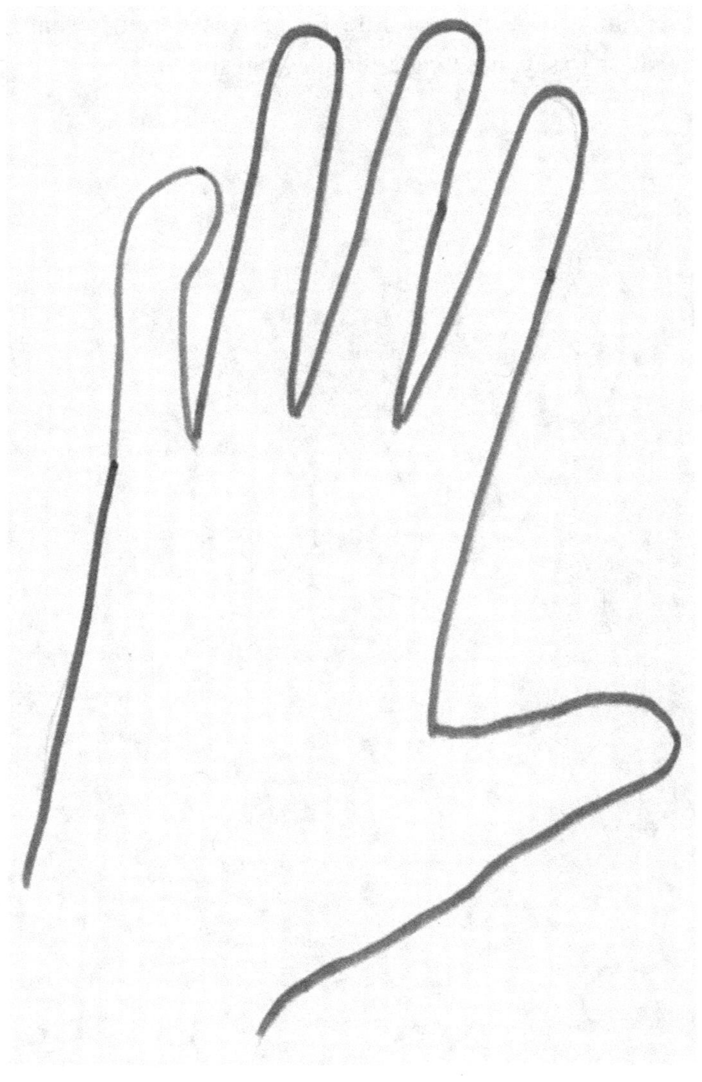

If the Jupiter finger is short and the Apollo and Mercury finger is long – The insecurity the person feels can be overcome creatively in an oral sense, so even people who know them very well would not know this about them.

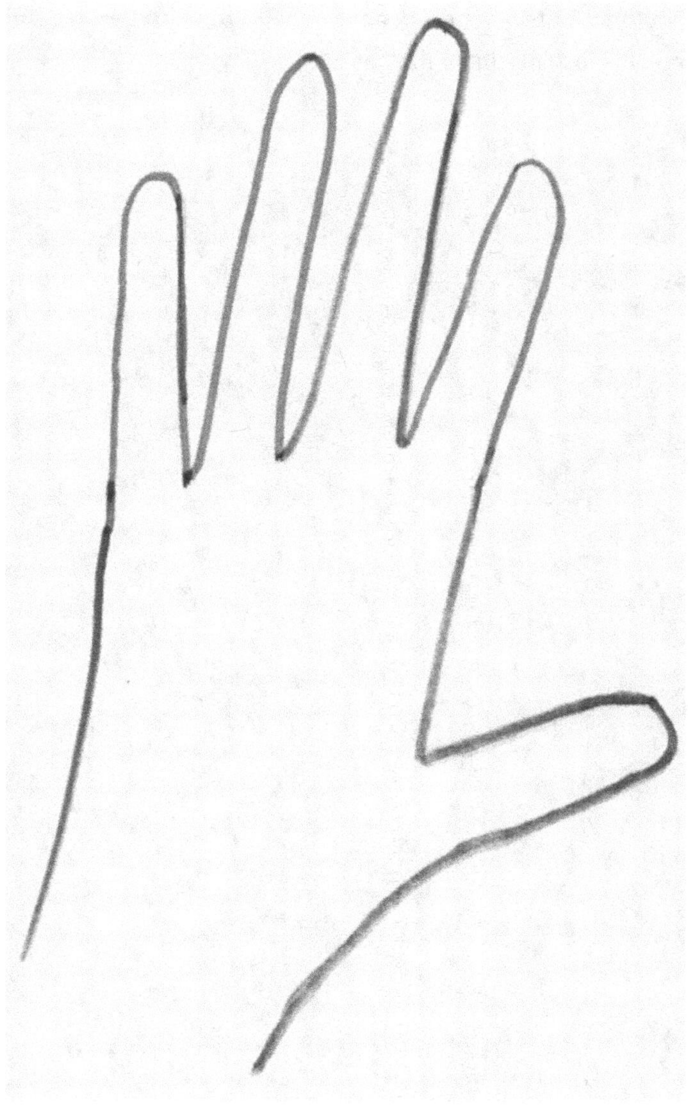

Mount

Large – A good communicator.

Medical stigmata – Three vertical lines found on the mount of Mercury.

Means health, as a subject, is important to the client. Doctors, nurses, and people who work in the healing industry usually have this marking.

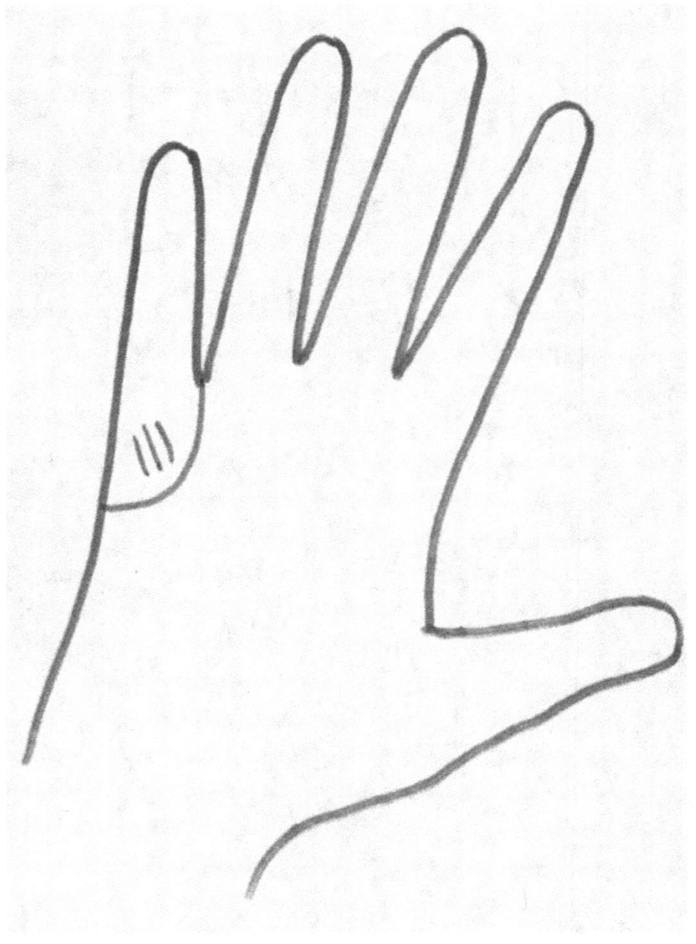

If there is a triangle on the mount – The person is learning another language at the time of the reading.

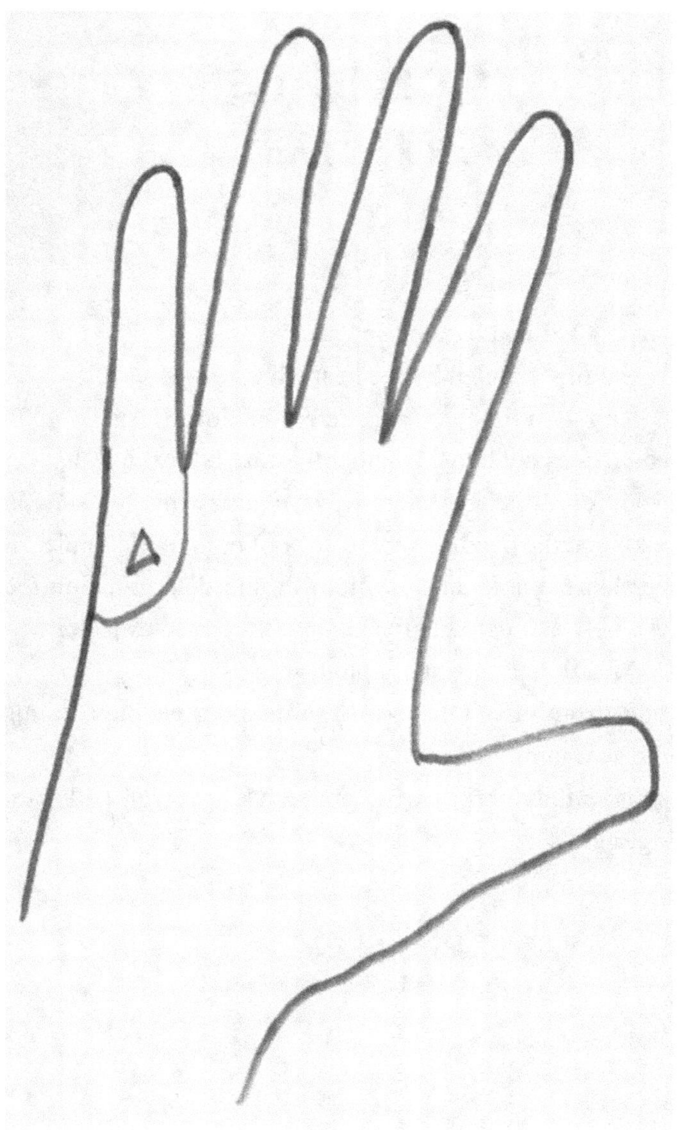

Chapter 5
The Thumb

Large – Is ruled by the head (a).

Small – Is ruled by the heart (b).

Top – Willpower and determination. (Usually if the person does not know whether they are left or right-handed, this is one of the easiest ways of knowing for sure, by looking at the padding on the back of both their thumbs and question the amount of willpower and determination they have now compared to the amount they used to.)

Middle – Logic and diplomacy.

Bottom – Compassion towards other people (can also represent family).

The thumbprint will sometimes override all other fingerprints.

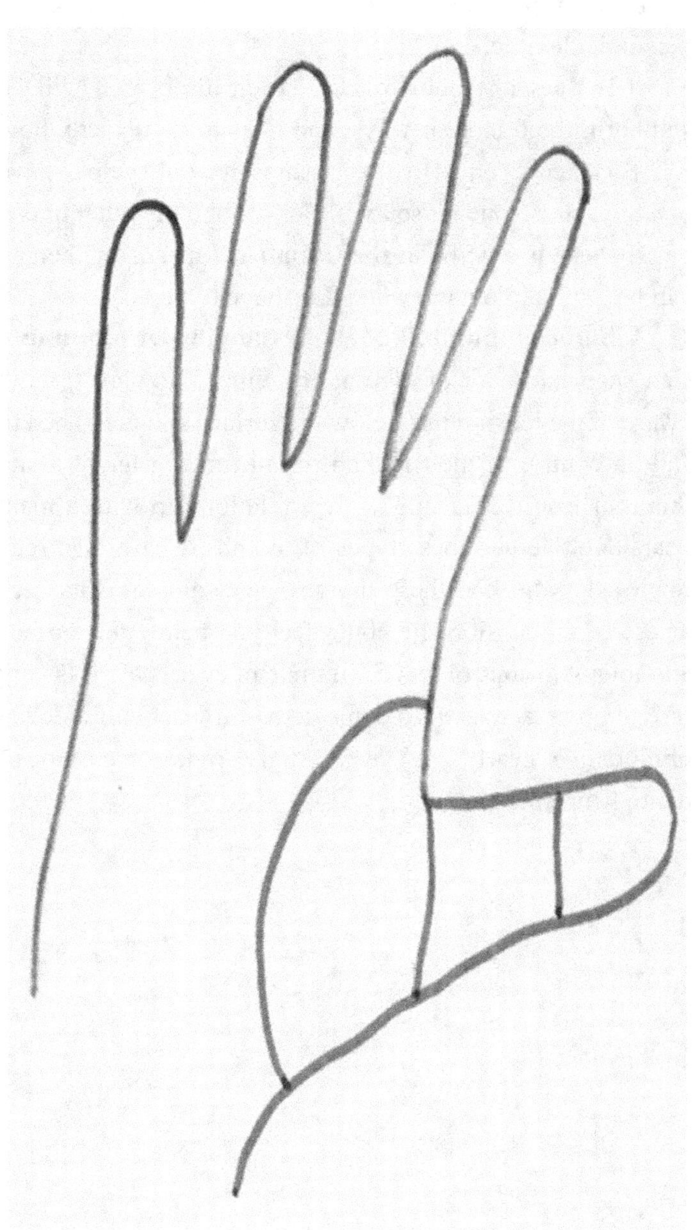

If the top of the thumb bends back – It means the person is flexible. (c)

If it does not bend back – Then the person will be stubborn, fixed in their ways, and likes to say exactly how it is. So when it comes to relationships, it would help to have one of each, so one person will flex around the other one.

If there is a waist in the thumb – It means the person can be quite diplomatic when they have to be. (d)

A bulbous thumb, known as the murder's thumb – Can snap into a fit of rage at any time. They are usually aware of the tension just below the surface and they need to stay in control of their feelings at all times. I learnt about this trait from being in a violent relationship with a man, years ago. He had these types of thumbs. I have also read for a lady who had these thumbs. She said she was very aware of the tension she could feel just below the surface and fought to control it every minute of every day. It is very rare to come across. I've come across at least half a dozen or more over nearly forty years. Angry Anderson has one of them, hence the name. (e)

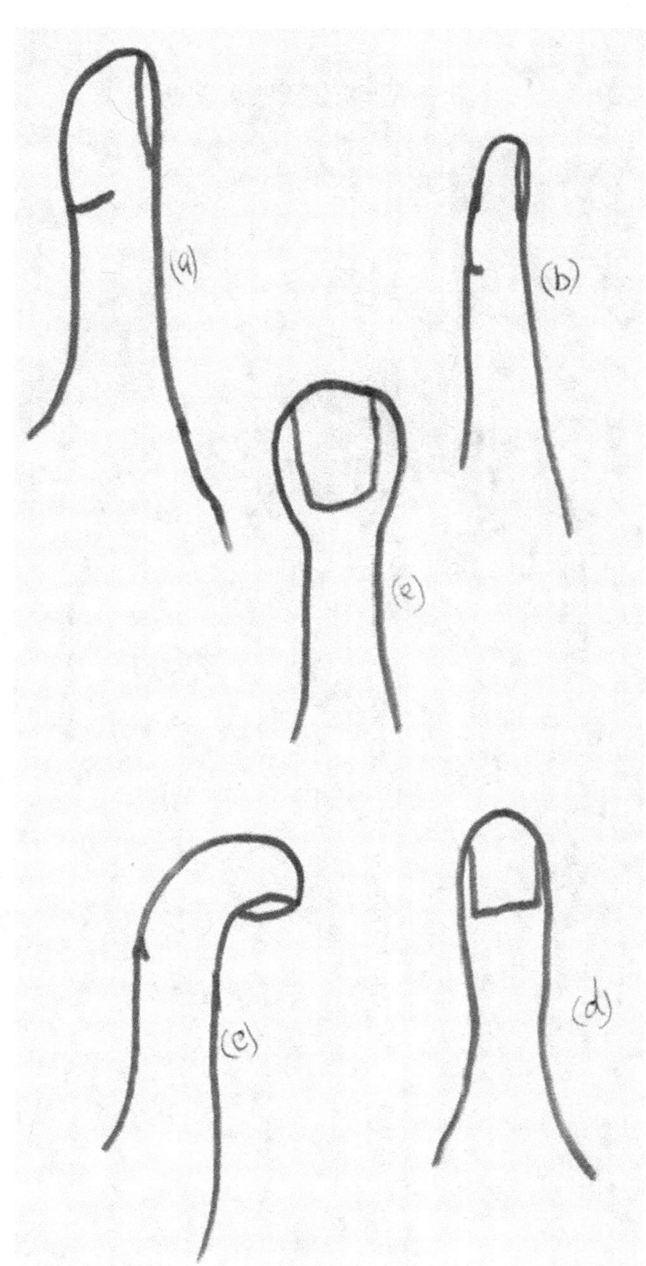
(a)
(b)
(e)
(c)
(d)

Gap between the Thumb and Jupiter

Low-set

Wide – Is an open and generous person.

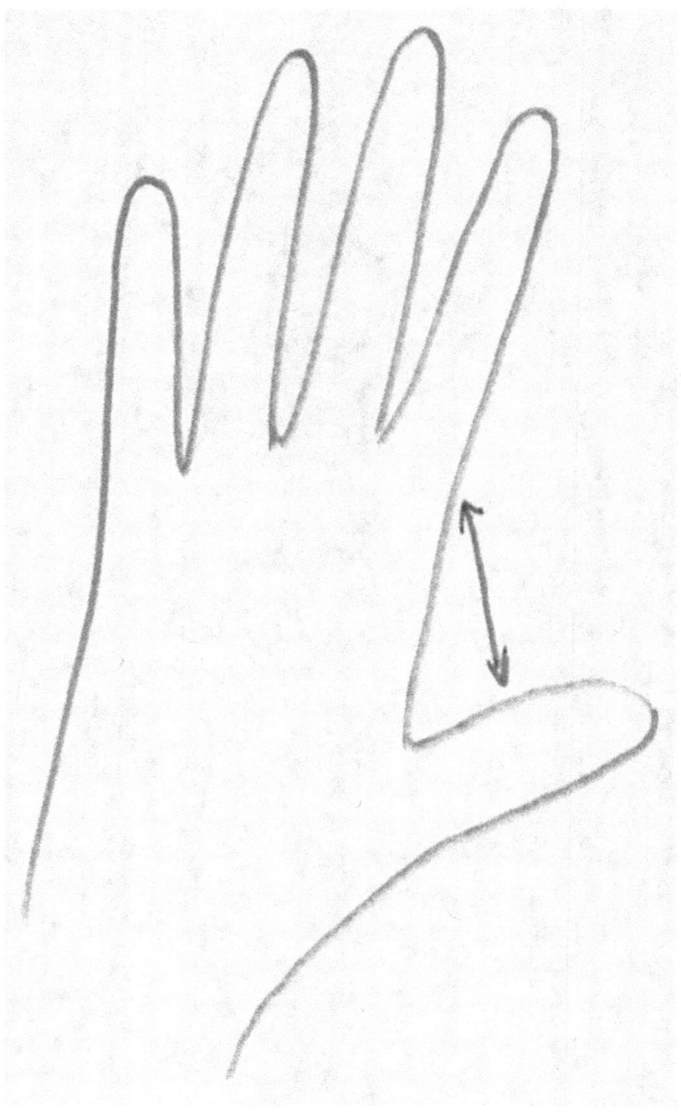

High-set

Narrow – Shy and self-protective.

Check both hands, may have changed over time.

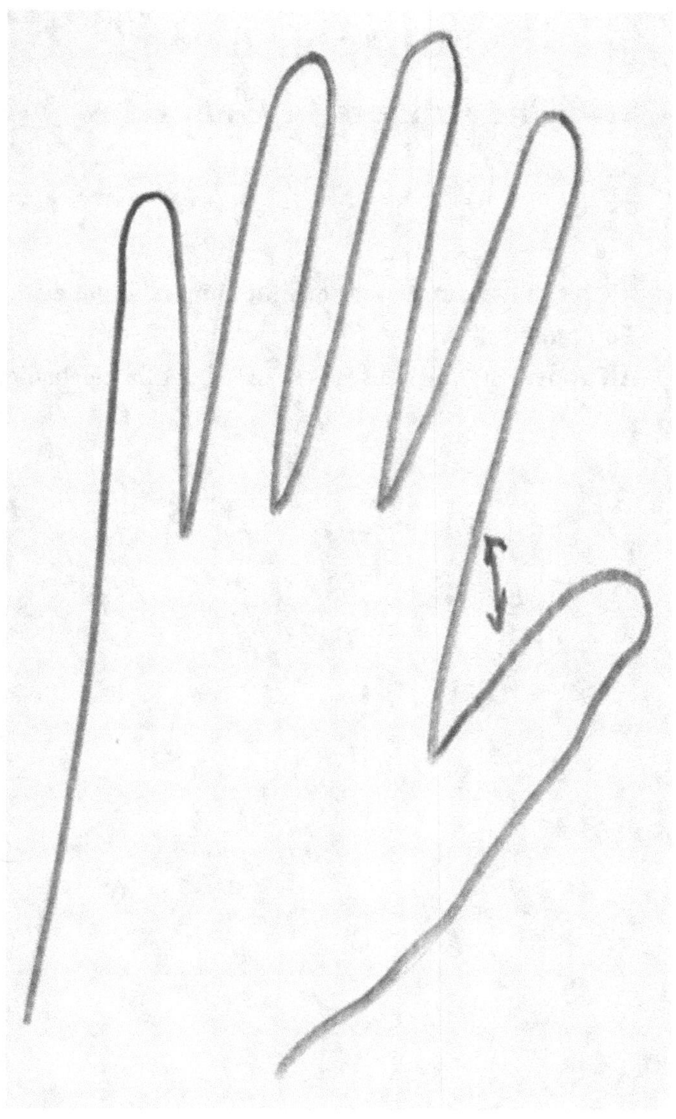

Chapter 6
The Fingers in General

A little bit of information about the fingers in general.

  Top phalanges

  All appearing bulbous – Is a sure sign of a mechanic.

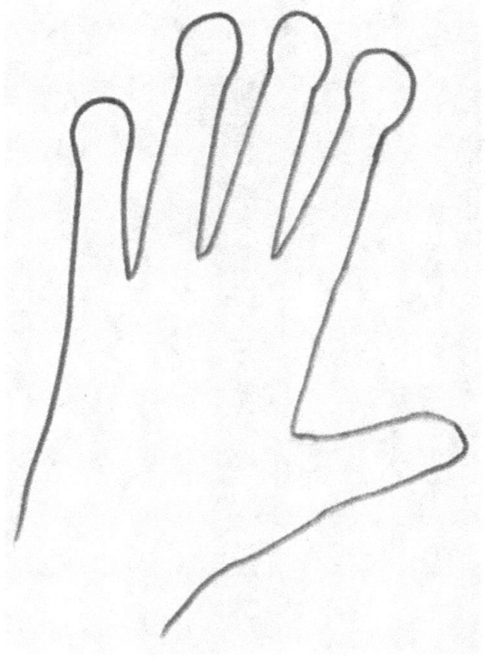

All having little bumps on them – Means the person loves their music.

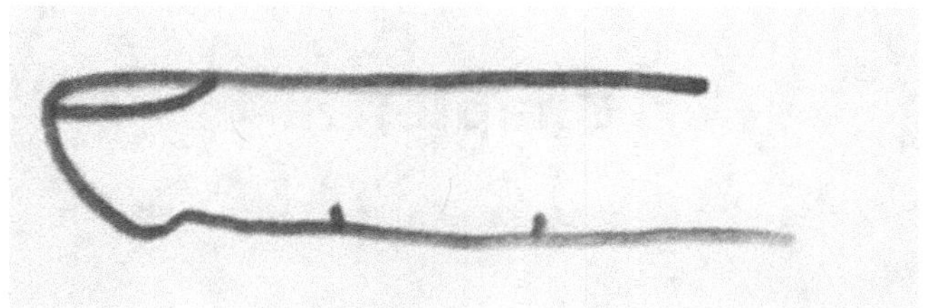

All appearing flat on the palm side – This is hard to show in a picture, so I will attempt to explain what I mean. When the palm has been faced down on the table and is then turned over, the skin on the top phalange does not bounce back. It is soft, almost fragile, and flat to look at. This is a sure sign of a gardener.

All the fingers splayed out like children do – Means they do have a child-like nature, and money is slipping straight through their fingers.

Finger lengths

Unusually long fingers – They are people who fuss over small details, particular about all that they do, so they are perfectionists.

Short fingers – Quick-thinking, impulsive person. A natural impatience to want things done yesterday. But if you know this about yourself, you can be much more understanding towards yourself.

Chapter 7

Puffy, Thick Bottom Joints

Show that the person likes to indulge in the luxuries of life.

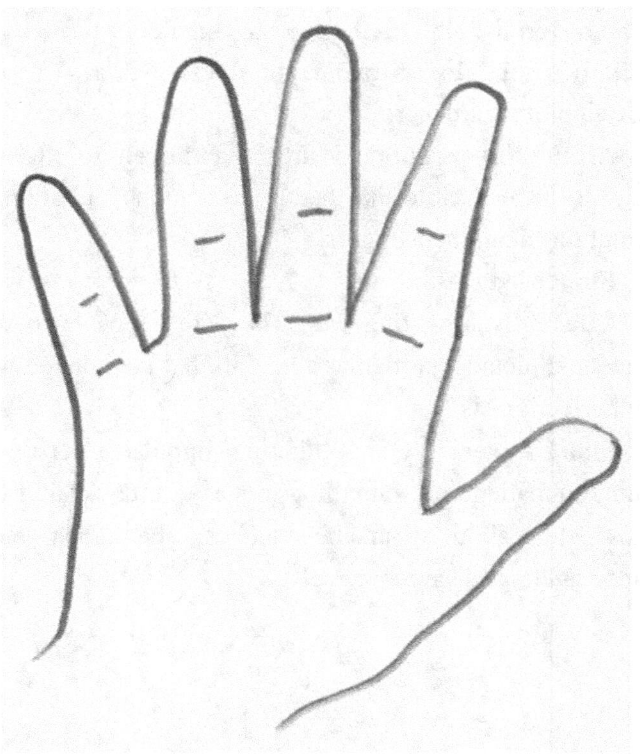

Thin Bottom Joints

Fussy about what they put into their bodies and avoid self-indulgence.

Smooth Fingers

Have a quick intuitive way of thinking. So they can think on their feet so to speak. Doesn't like arguments, also tends to blurt out exactly what's on their mind without giving it too much thought. As a result, they tend to be dealing with things as they go instead of bottling things up.

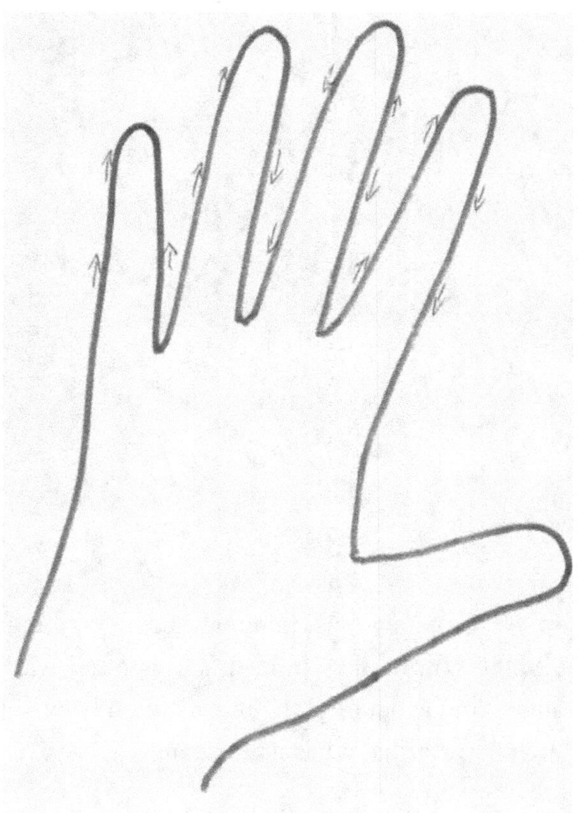

Knotty Knuckles

Shows a mind that loves to argue and reason things out. Slow and deliberate person.

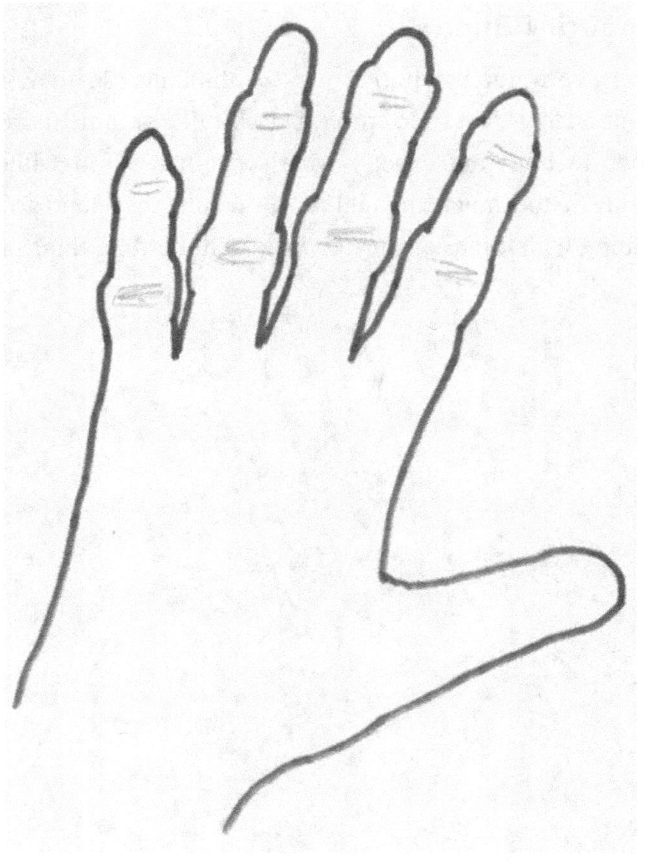

Top – Thoroughly must think through everything.

Bottom – Knows how to keep a secret and will know when something is out of place on a material level.

Watch for arthritis, it has no meaning.

Angle of Dexterity

Will jump up and do what needs doing when it needs doing. So, very agile.

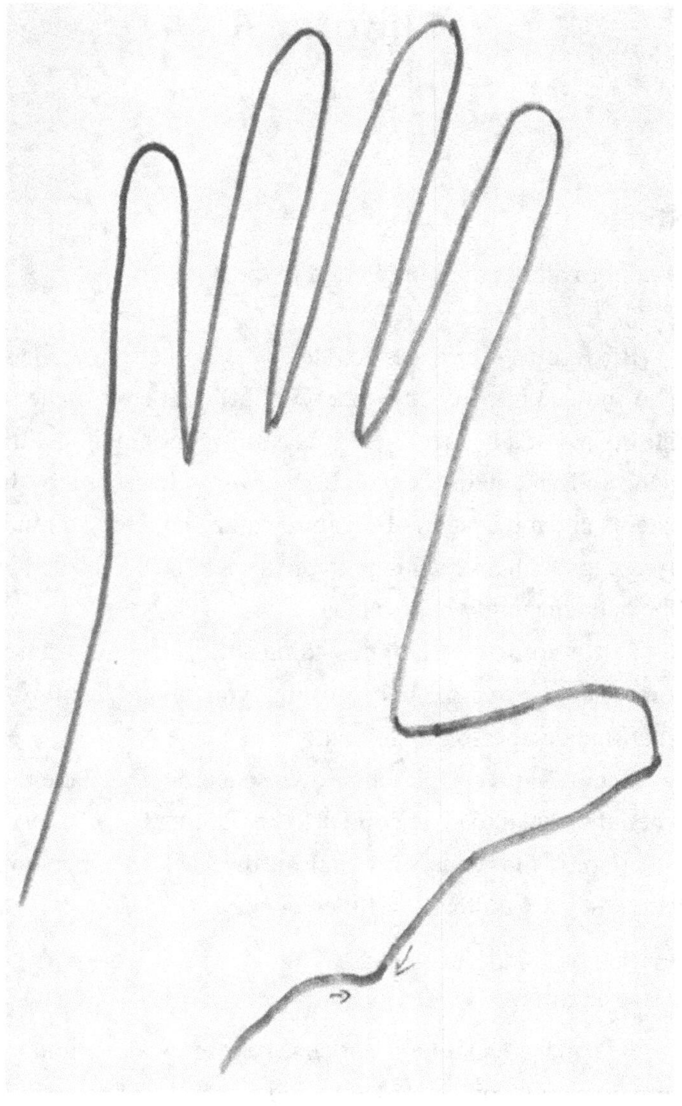

Chapter 8

Size

Big, normal, or small in relation to the body.

Big hands – Intricate, detailed work. I once knew a lady who showed me this little tree with different eggs made up into rooms of a house. There was a music room with a little piano and a mantelpiece with flowers on. A bedroom for the parents and a teenager's bedroom, bathroom, etc., all made from eggs with a little hinge to open each one to see inside. She had amazingly huge hands.

Little hands – Do big things. So, if you wanted someone to organize a big event, you would employ a small-handed person to do that.

Broad hands – Like their own space. So they take that when they need to. They prefer to be outdoors.

Also, if the veins show out on the back of a person's hand, they are quite a sensitive person.

Fingernails

Spatulate – Outdoor workers, very innovative, good at coming up with original ideas, good at mending and making things. Have a lot of excess energy. Love to be out in nature. Always found on tradesmen hands.

Broad nails – Broad-minded. (b)

Straight, narrow nails – Indoor workers, happy to admire nature from the window. The only exception is the gardener. (c)

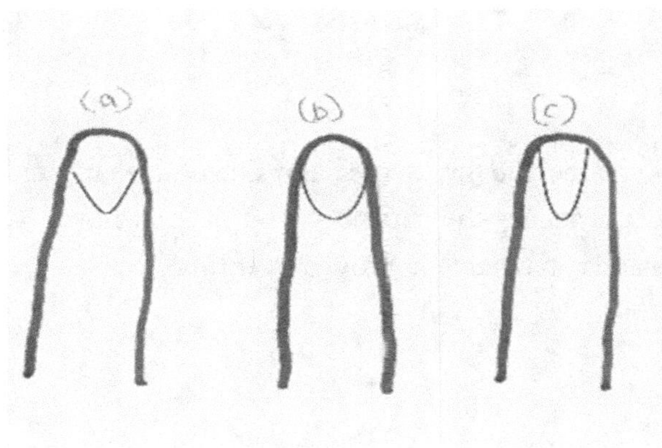

Short nails – Means short-tempered.

Chewed fingernails – Means the person has a nervous disposition.

Fingertips

Relate to the finger it is found on.

Spatulate – Means the same as the spatulate nail. (a)

Squared – Means the person has a set way of doing things. (b)

Conic (or rounded) – Social, easy-going, intuitive people. (c)

Pointed – Spiritual type of mind (very rare). (d)

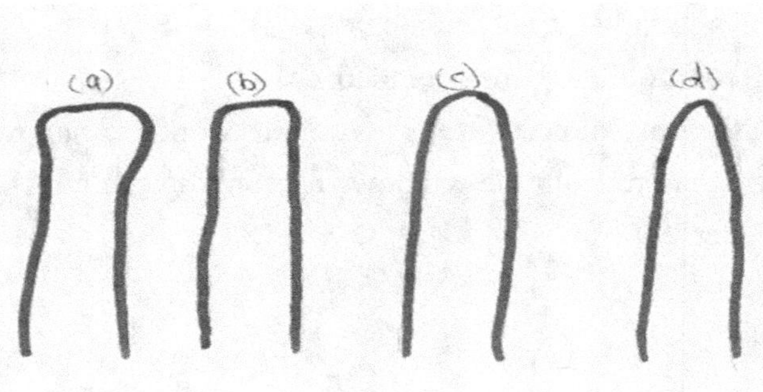

If you feel the tips on the palm side of the hand and they are soft, it means the person is a bit of a pushover. Check both hands, may have improved over time.

Chapter 9
Hands Shapes

Earth Hands

Palm is square and fingers are short. Practical, hardworking, and reliable, likes to just concentrate on one thing at a time. Dislikes change. Has a special connection with nature, which makes their energy calming and good to be around. Most farmers and factory workers have earth hands.

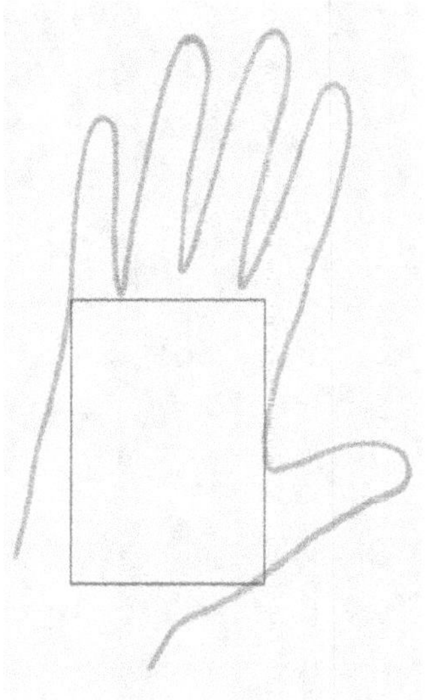

Water Hands

Palm is rectangular and the fingers are long. Very common among actresses and models. Graceful, sensitive, refined-natured people who can be easily swayed by people and situations. Emotions are very important to these people. They can do well with a good support network. Indicates intelligence in a male.

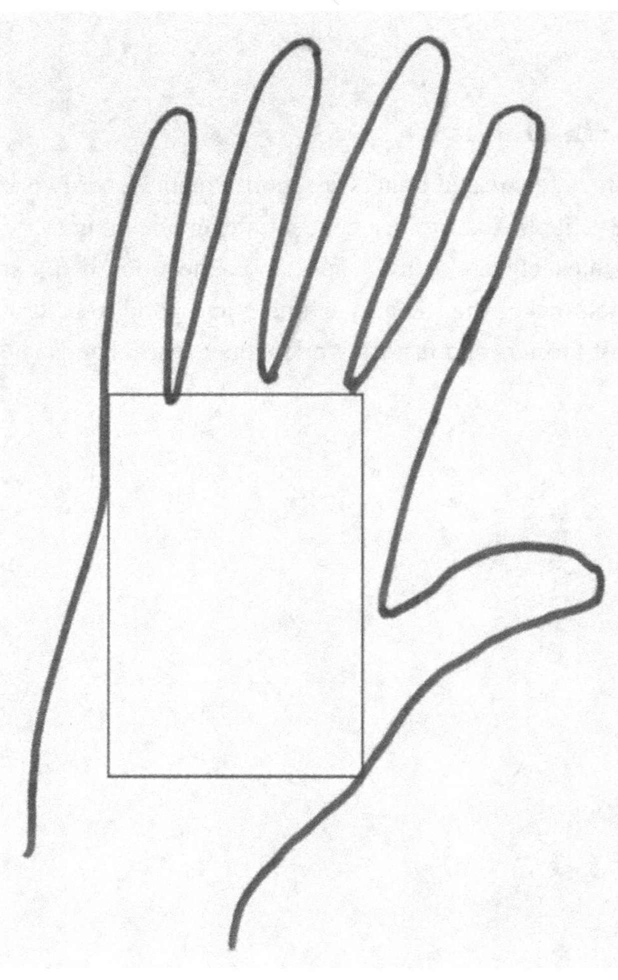

Fire Hands

The palm is rectangular and the fingers are short. These people are always on the go. They are very passionate people. They know how to sway people and control situations to their way of thinking. Many of our world leaders have this type of hand shape, e.g. Donald Trump (President of the United States) and Scott Morrison (Prime Minister of Australia).

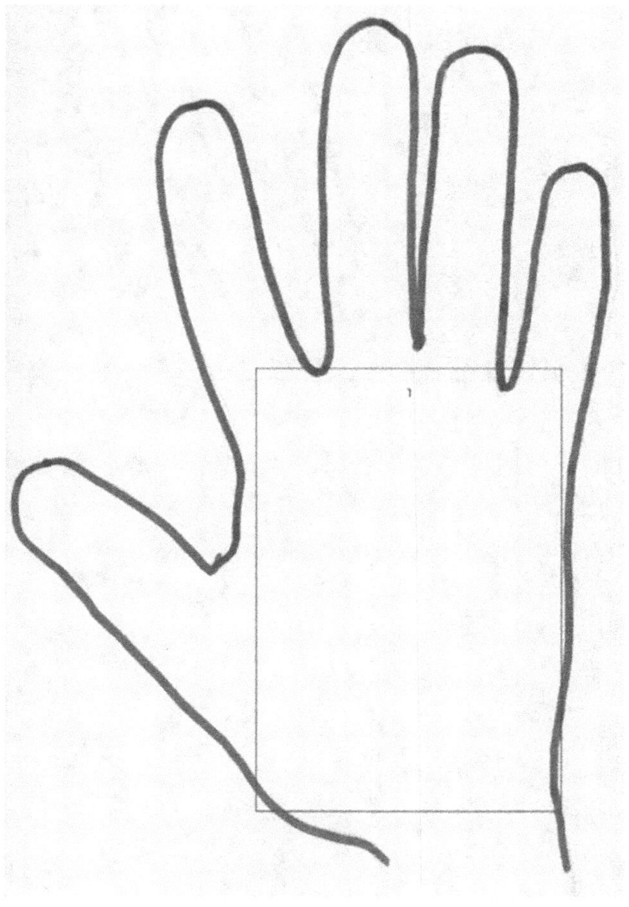

Air Hands

The palm is square and the fingers are long. These people love to learn and are very good with communication. Suited to radio, reporting, and other media jobs. Knows how to control their emotions. Mentally active and loves to talk. Also pays attention to detail.

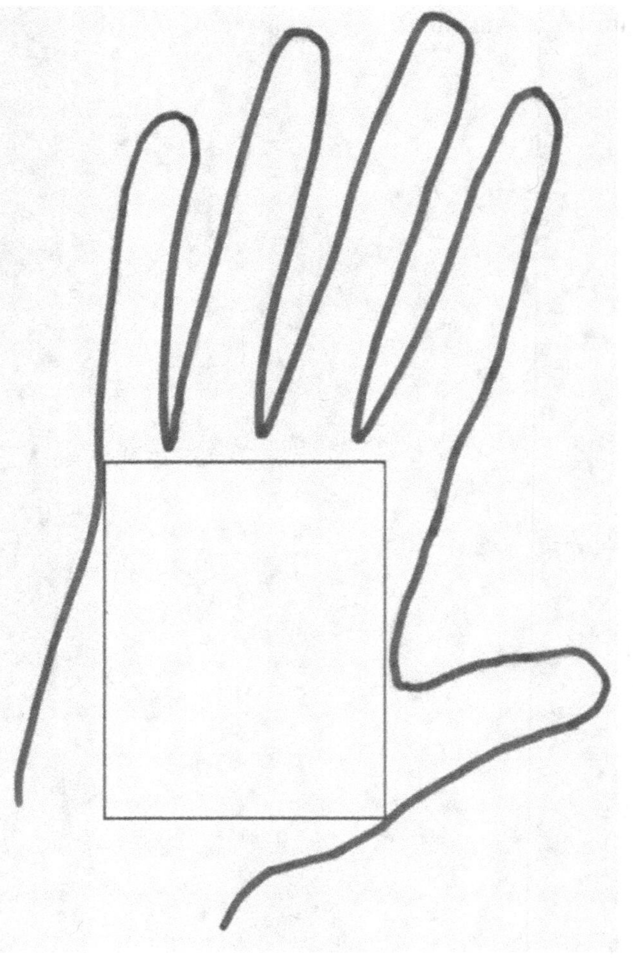

Chapter 10

Procrastination Lines

This is the hand of a lady who has been procrastinating over a change in her career, so she has procrastination lines on her Jupiter finger which is associated with her personal ambition and goals. The top one means she needs to speak up about what she wants to do, the middle one has to do with business, and the bottom one is doing something about it in a practical sense. The middle finger is to do with work, and the middle phalange on the little finger is to do with getting organized. She has also got them on the top phalange of the thumb, which means she has been determined to procrastinate. The reason we get procrastination lines is if we are meant to do something but we don't, that's when we get them. If we continue to procrastinate, the lines will get deeper and darker and harder to get rid of. So really, these are a temporary thing. I usually mention these at the end of the reading, because by that time, I know what they have been procrastinating about. Which in turn helps them to move on with their life.

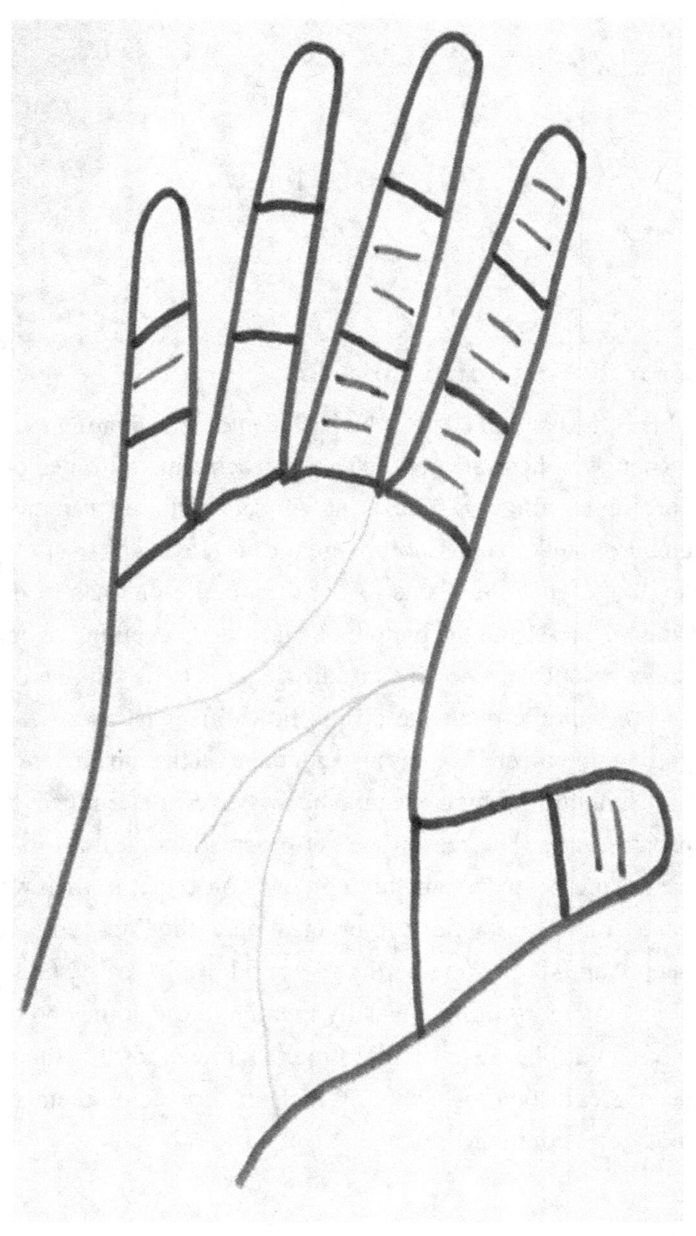

Texture

Hard – Hard on themselves and other people at times.

Soft – Has a few different meanings. You would have to ask the client which one suits them.

- Hormones.
- Not well.
- Pregnant.
- Or just plain lazy.
- Gardeners also have really soft, almost fragile skin on the palm side of the hand, as we have already mentioned.

Freckles, Moles, and Warts

Means an emotional blockage in whichever the place it is found on the hand. For an example, say a lady has had a lot of trouble getting pregnant, only to have miscarried twice and had an ectopic pregnancy, she might have a freckle on the Neptune mount.

Scars – Means the person is scared in that area of their life. For example, the person had a scar on the bottom thumb phalange, it would mean they have been scarred in the area of family for some reason.

Temperament

Warm or cool to the touch would relate to the temperament. Sweaty hands mean they have a nervous temperament.

Chapter 11
Skin Ridge Patterns

Skin Ridge Patterns – Are like fingerprints but can be found on different parts of the palms. Always look at both hands, they are not always present. These do not come and go, like fingerprints. You are born with them.

Between the Apollo and Mercury fingers – This shows a good sense of humor and a love of animals. A whorl in the same area as the loop of humor, definitely means an animal lover. (a)

Between the Mercury and Apollo fingers – Is the loop of style. This shows good dress sense and an eye for color and décor. This can also indicate vanity. Some people have both a loop of humor and a loop of style. (b)

Between Saturn and Apollo fingers – The loop of serious intent. It means the person is serious with what they set out to do in life and this can make a person successful all by itself. (c)

At the end of the head line – It means the person is good with telepathy. (d)

On Luna – The Luna loop. This signifies a love of the countryside and of nature. Will eventually move to the country if they are not there already.

Between the Jupiter and Saturn fingers – The Rajah loop. This means that the person has royal blood running through his veins. The royalty may be Asian, European, or anything else. But if the loop is there, the blue blood is also there.

The Rajah loop is rare on even one hand, but extremely rare on both hands, meaning, no doubt about royalty. I have only ever seen it a few times in the last 30 odd years. The first time was a lady and her daughter; each had one on the less dominant hand, which meant somewhere in their family tree, there was royalty. Two brothers had it on both hands, they were royalty in the east somewhere. Also a friend was telling me about the stories of royalty in the family that her mother used to tell her about when she was young, that she was not sure to believe and when I looked into her palms, she had one on both of her hands and recently checked her daughters and grandchildren and they all had them as well. She was pleasantly surprised to know that all the stories were true after all. (f)

Charisma – It belongs to a very charismatic person. (g)

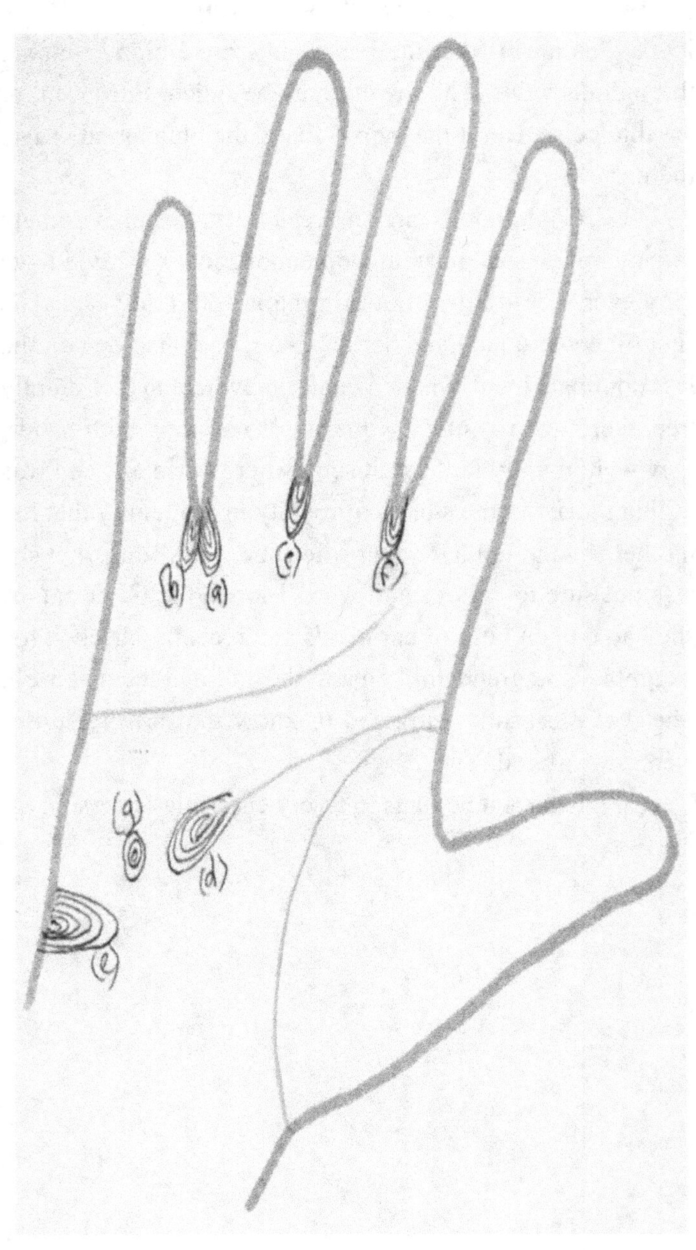

(b)
(a)
(c)
(f)
(g)
(d)
(e)

Chapter 12
Fingerprints

The Whorl – Very much an individual. Thoughtful and intense. Knows how to keep things to themselves. Often talented in some way. Ideas and opinions will be fully thought through before they put them out there. They can sometimes get so consumed in what they are doing that the whole world seems to disappear around them. (a)

The Arch – A practical person. Good at making and mending things, good with the hands in general. Suspicious, needs proof, must be able to see to believe, and is the reason I like to point out where the information is coming from. Hard working and reliable. Likes to keep their emotions in reserve. (b)

The Tented Arch – With a pole shows enthusiasm, becomes deeply involved in everything they do. (c)

Loops – Very much a people person, likeable, sociable, and gets along well with other people. Also, good at making the best out of any situation. Well balanced, middle-of-the-road type people. (d)

A Double Loop – Means indecision. Two sides to everything. I usually tell the person to go with the very first thing they thought of when they were not thinking, before they started arguing with themselves, because that is their intuition. (e)

How dark or light the fingerprints are due to the strength of the meaning. Also depends on which finger you find the prints on, it will vary the meaning, i.e., if found on the Saturn finger, it will pertain to the person's work.

The thumbprint overrides all the other fingerprints at times.

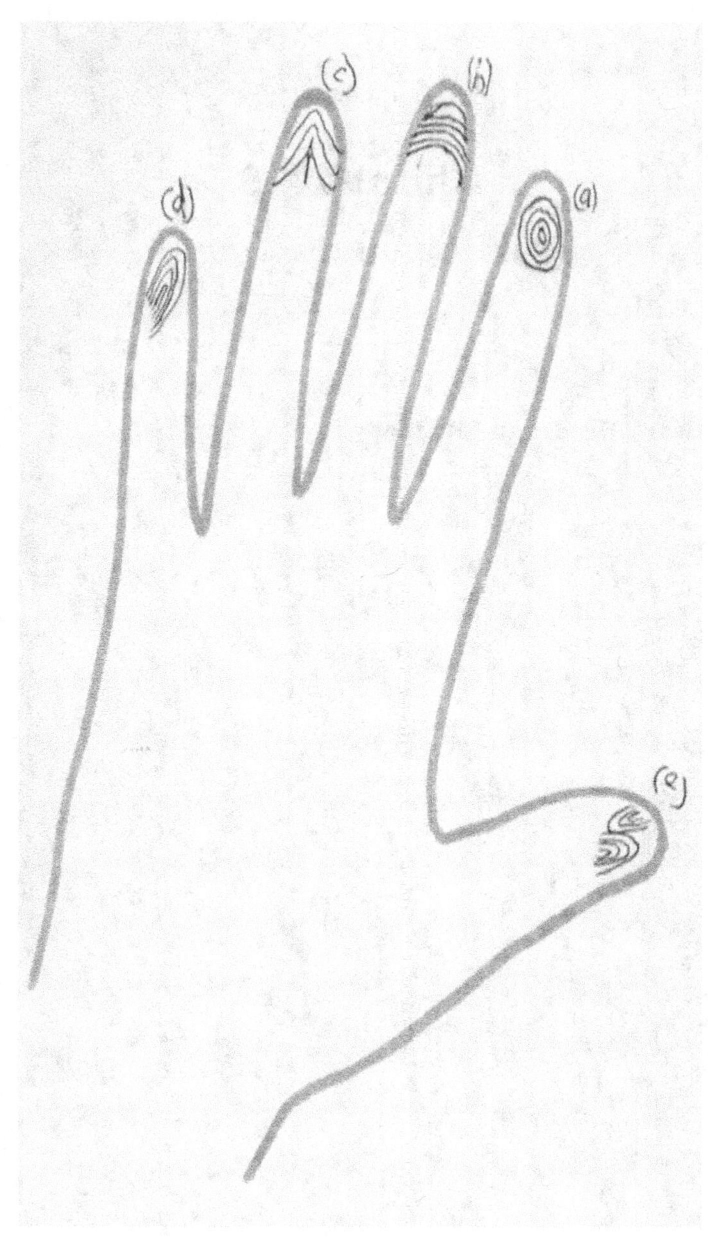
(c)
(b)
(d)
(a)
(e)

Chapter 13
Timing on the Hand

Heart, Head, and Life Lines

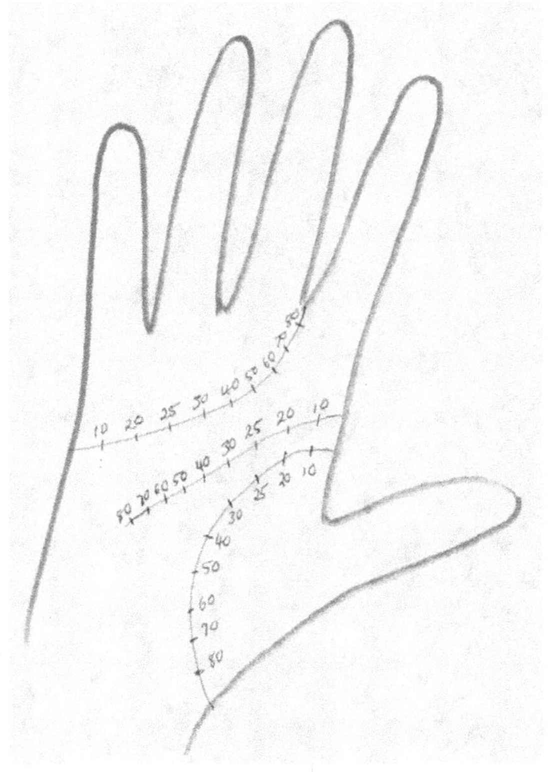

Fate (Work) Line and Line of the Sun

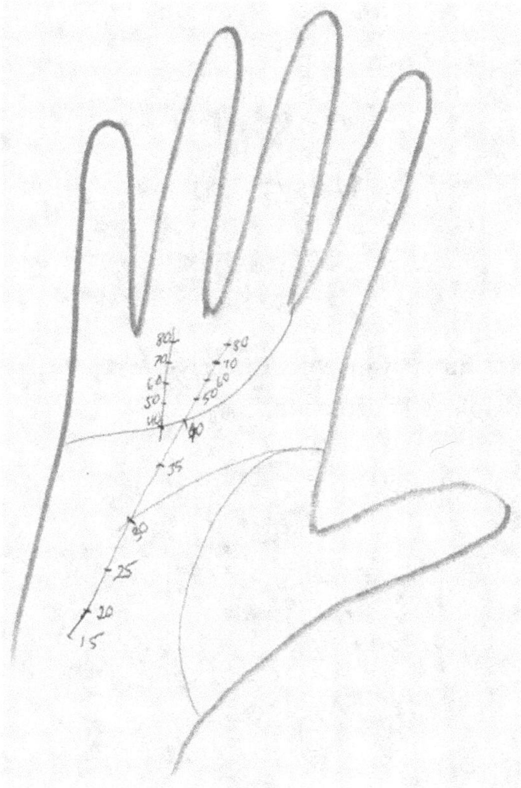

The heart line begins under the little finger, and the head and life start under the Jupiter finger. The fate (work) line, line of the sun, and the health and travel lines, all go from the base of the palm upwards.

There is an easy way of remembering. The head is thirty years of age and the heart line is forty years. Also, if you hung a bit of string from the gap between the Jupiter and Saturn fingers, that would be twenty-one years old on the head and life line.

Chapter 14
Heart Line

1. Knows how to give and receive love, doesn't mind public displays of affection.

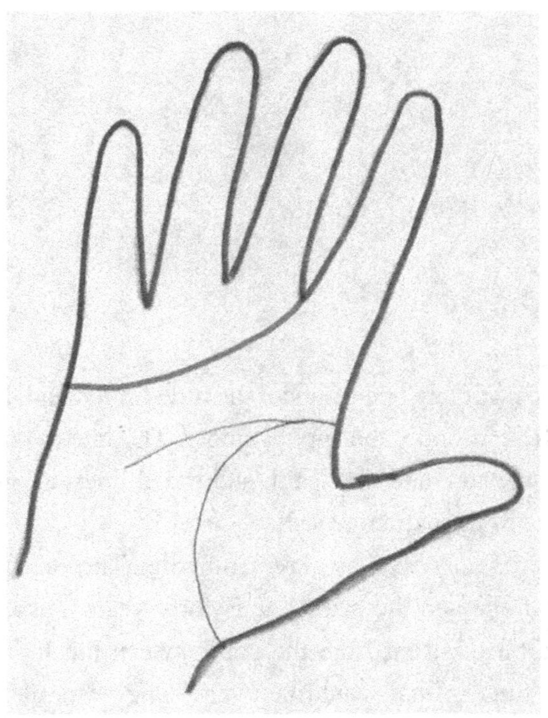

2. Humanitarian

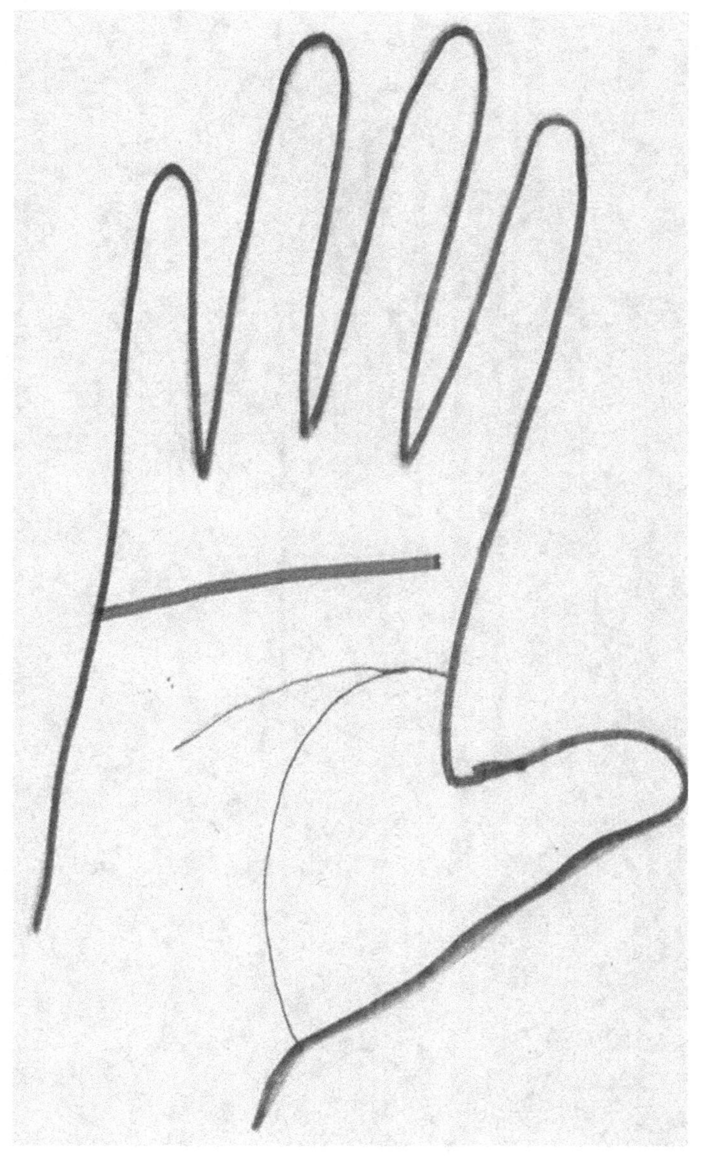

3. Has been hurt badly in the past, so is unlikely to hurt anybody else because they know how it feels.

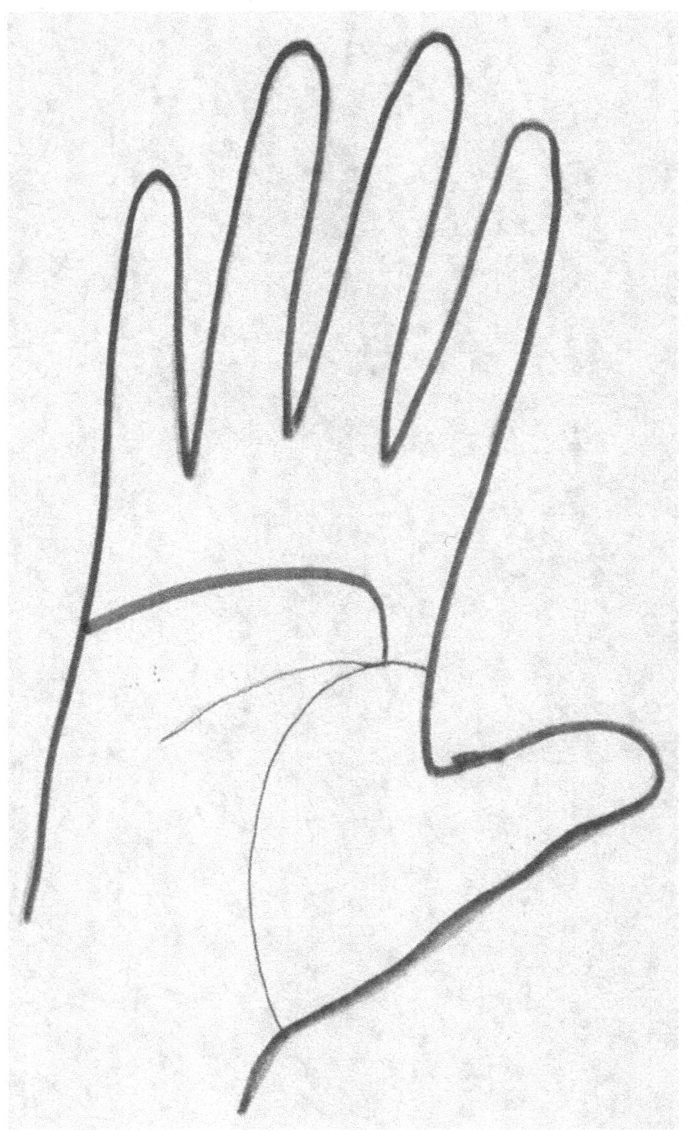

4. Reserved, can sit in a comfortable silence and just know that the love is there. Very fussy about their choice in a partner.

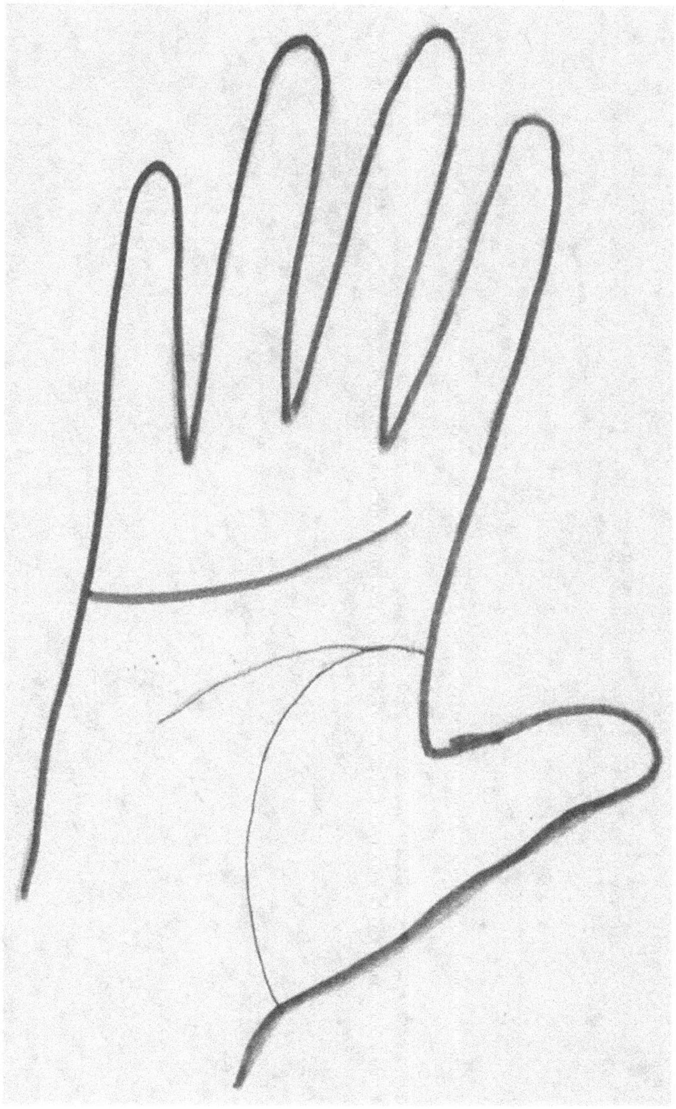

5. Short is only capable of a physical relationship.

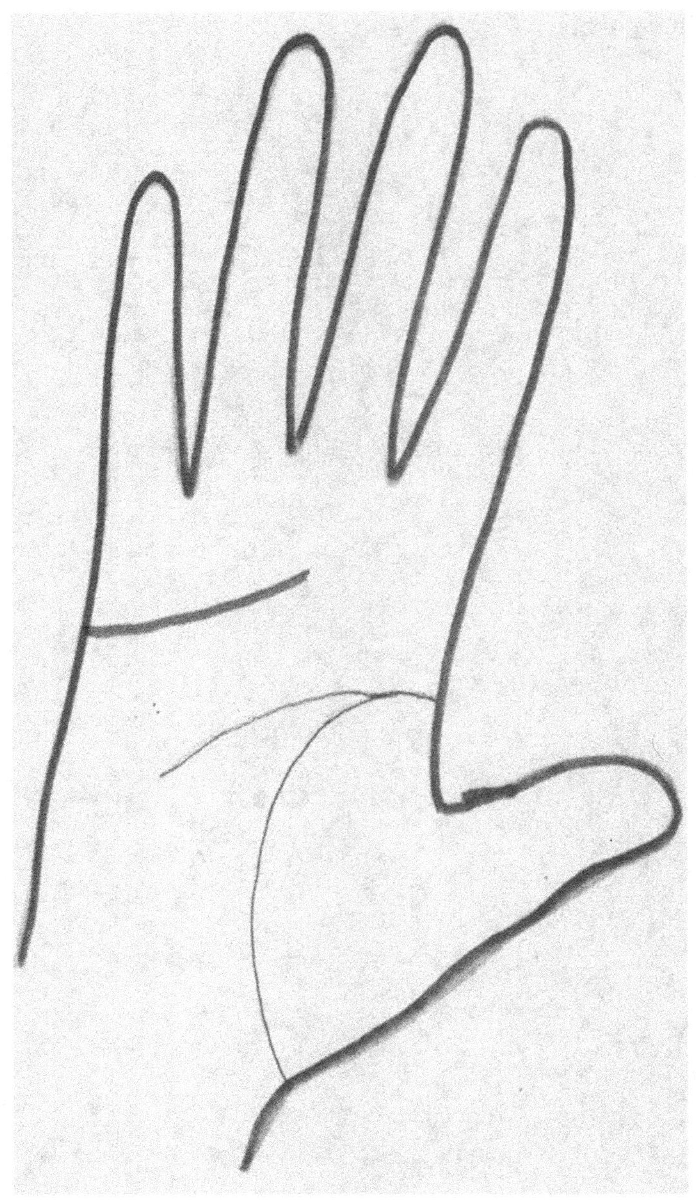

6. All three means the person is very emotionally complex. Check out both hands may only be on one hand.

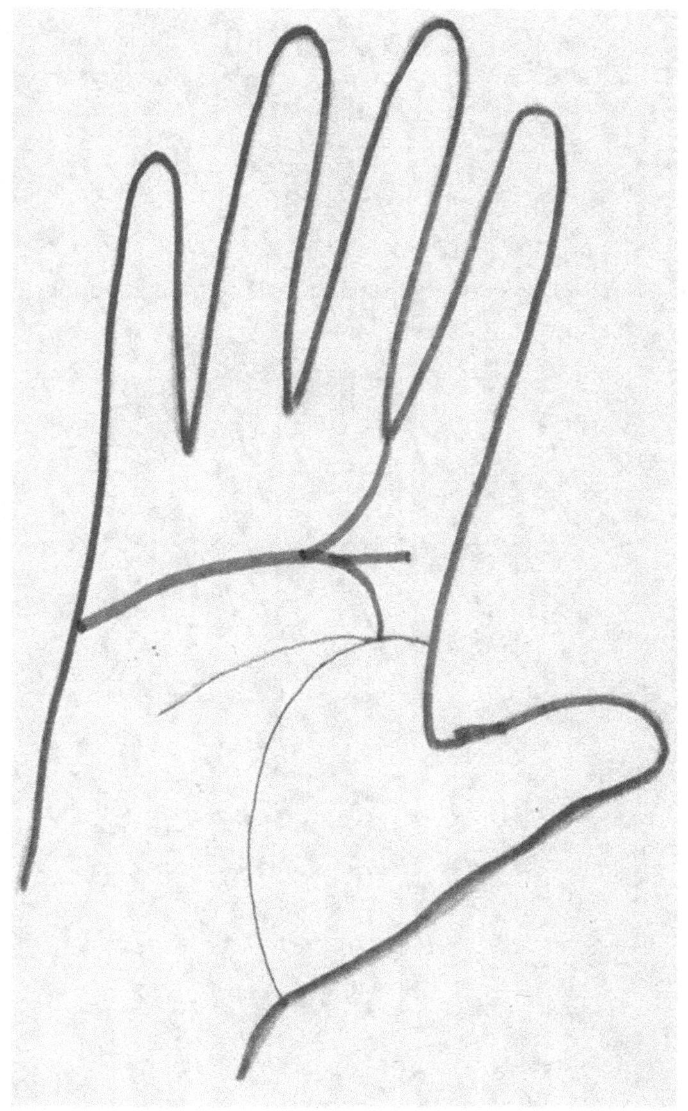

Chapter 15
Head Line

1. Short – Does not give too much thought to anything.

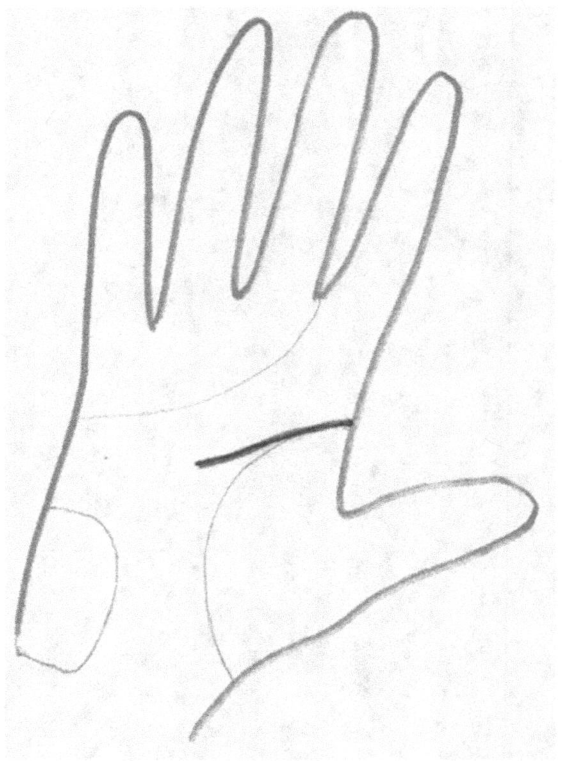

2. Long – Analytical and will never stop learning.

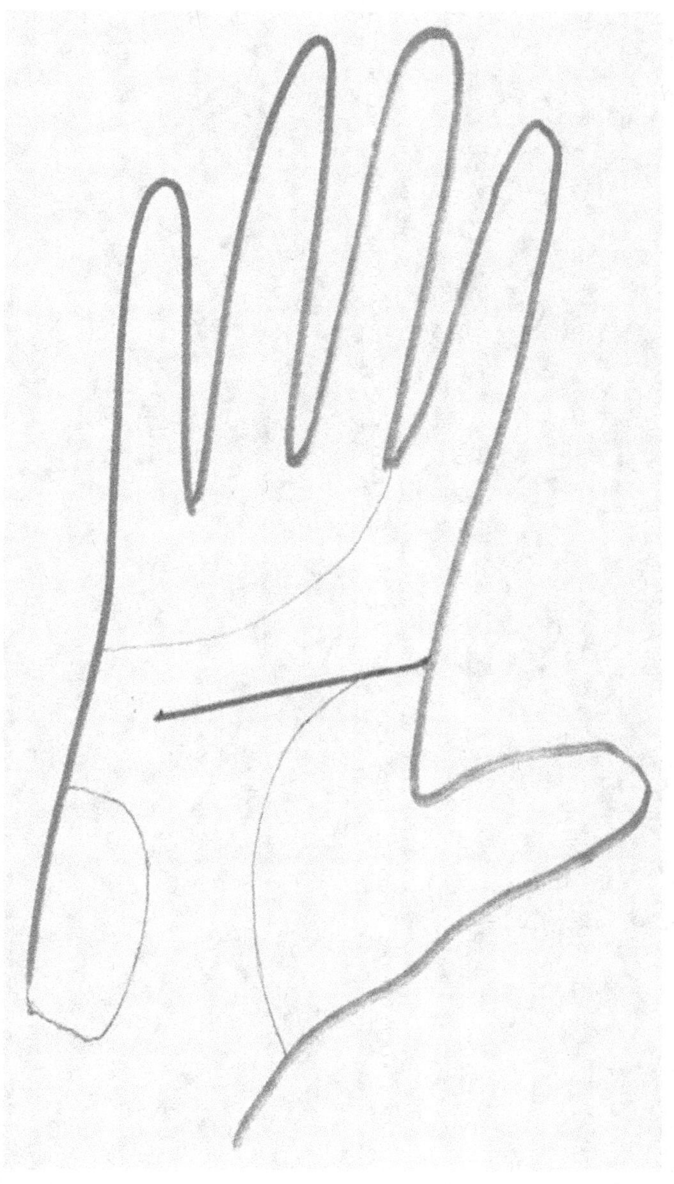

3. Straight – Sees everything in black and white. Good with math and computers.

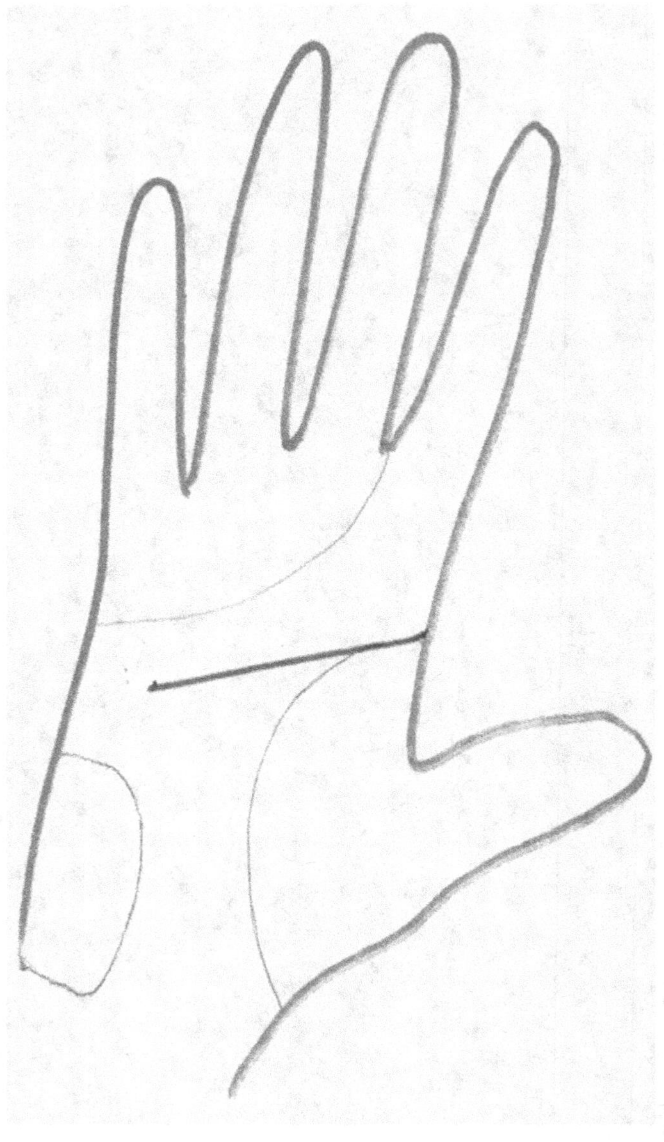

4. With a curve – Creativity and Imagination.

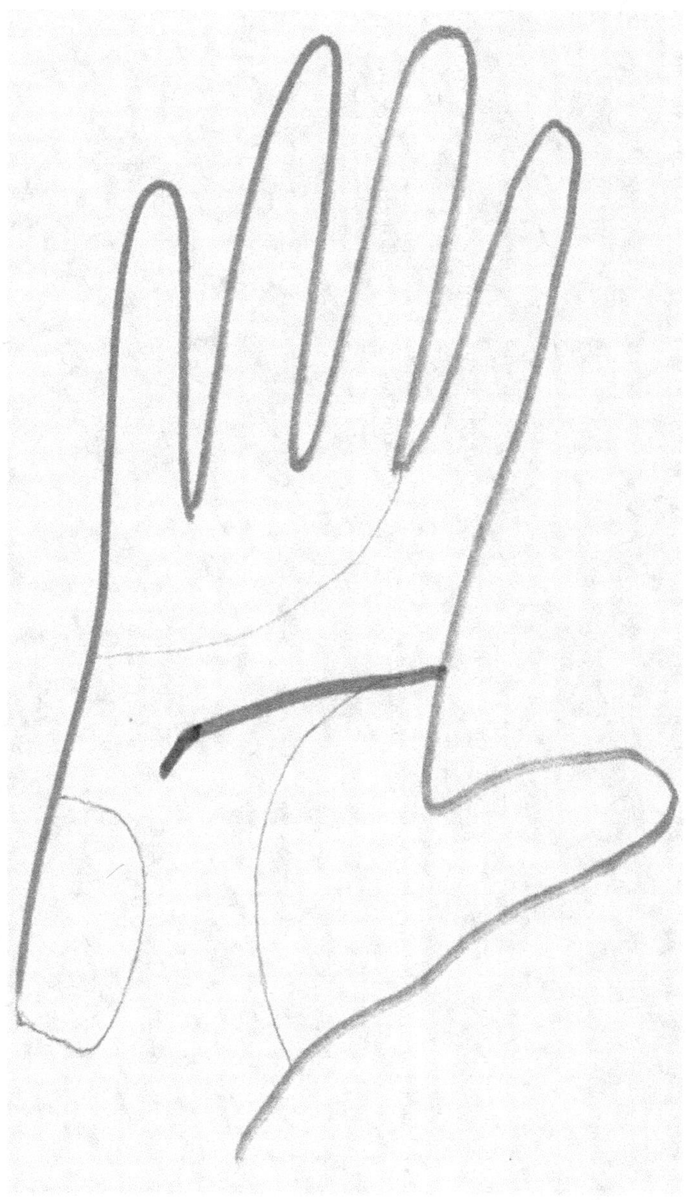

5. Ambitious – Starting on the Jupiter mount is a sign of ambition.

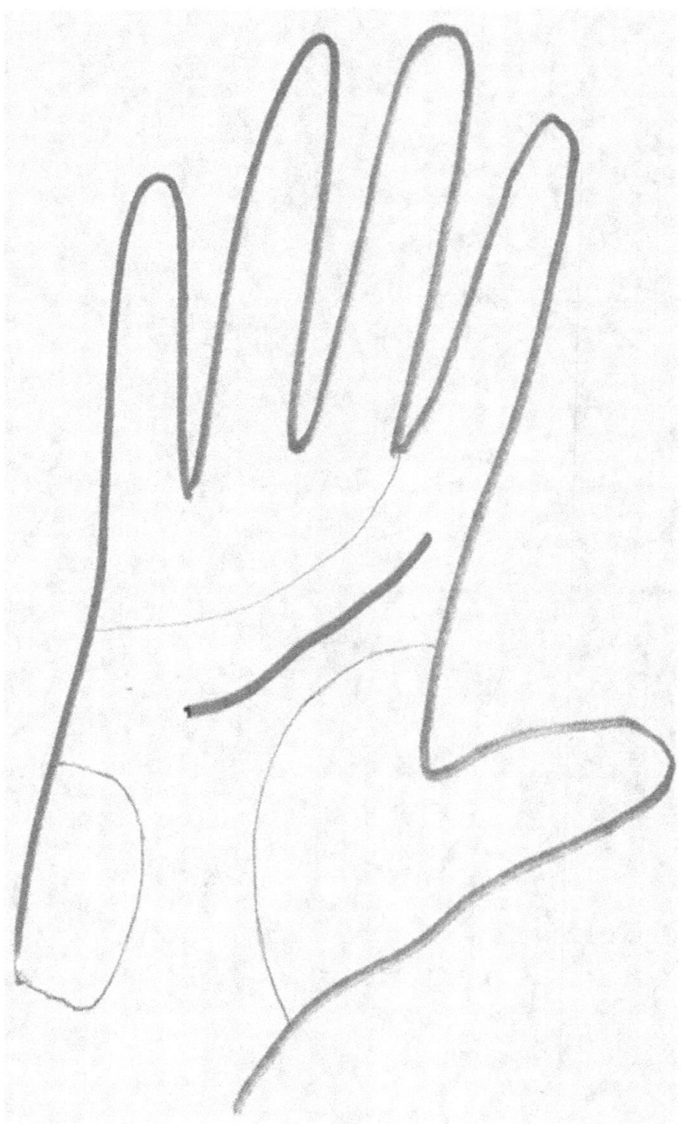

6. Depression – When the head line ends on the Luna mount, it looks like the person's imagination has got carried away with itself.

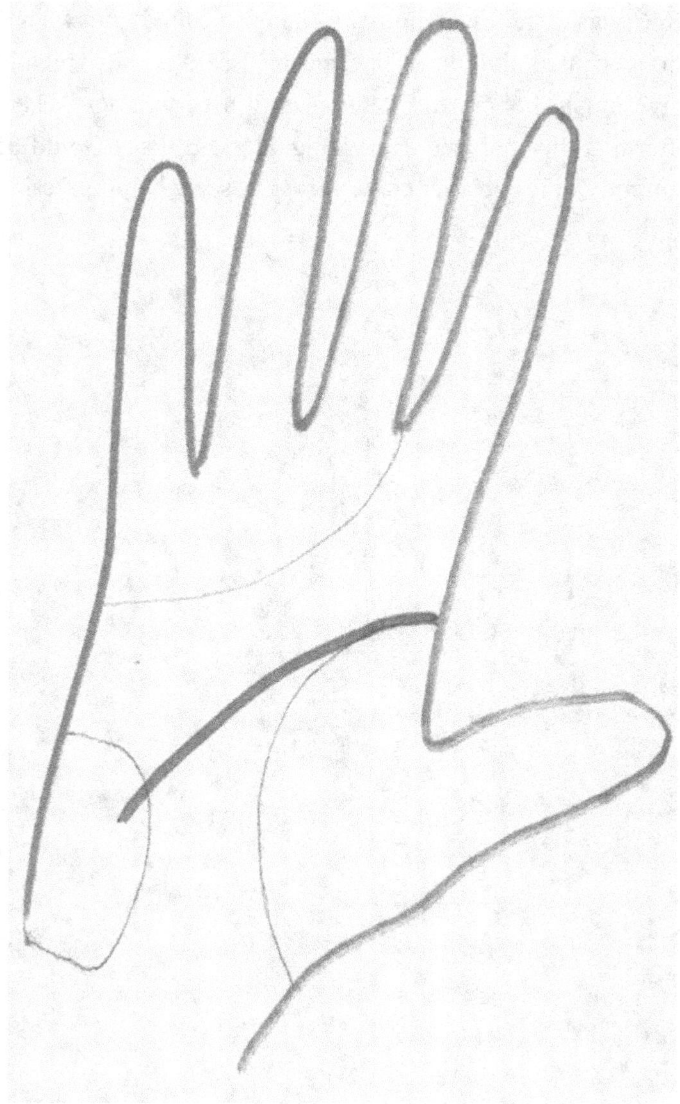

7. Double head line – I have only ever seen this twice over the last 30 odd years. The first time was a woman who wanted to share a workroom with me on alternating days. I declined the offer, so I never really got to know her. Another time was a fellow palmist. When he asked me what I thought his double head line meant, I said he never really gave much thought to anything until a certain age. Then, after that, he analyzed everything. He said that I would be correct. So, if you ever come across it, see what impression it gives you at the time.

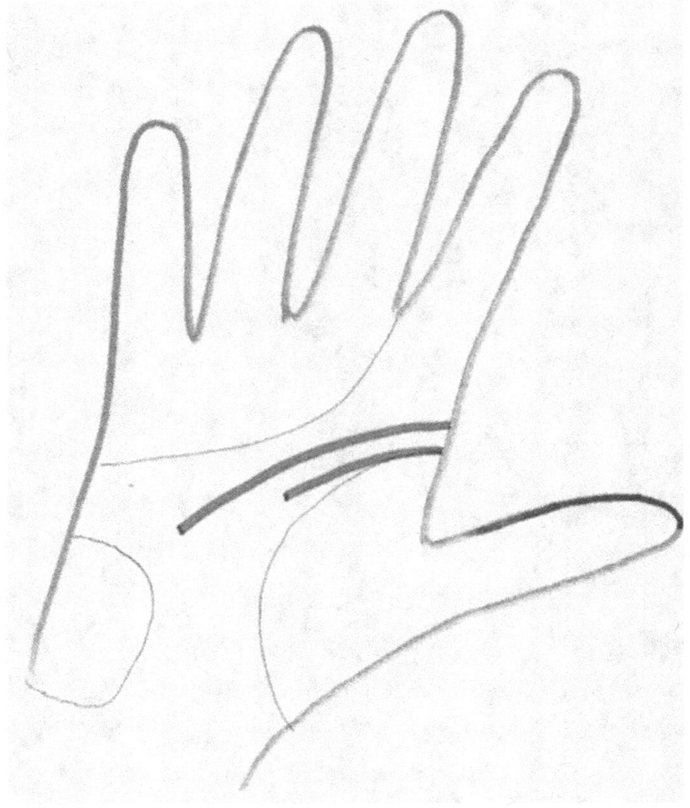

8. Separate to the life line – Independent thinking, feels independent enough to make their own decisions.

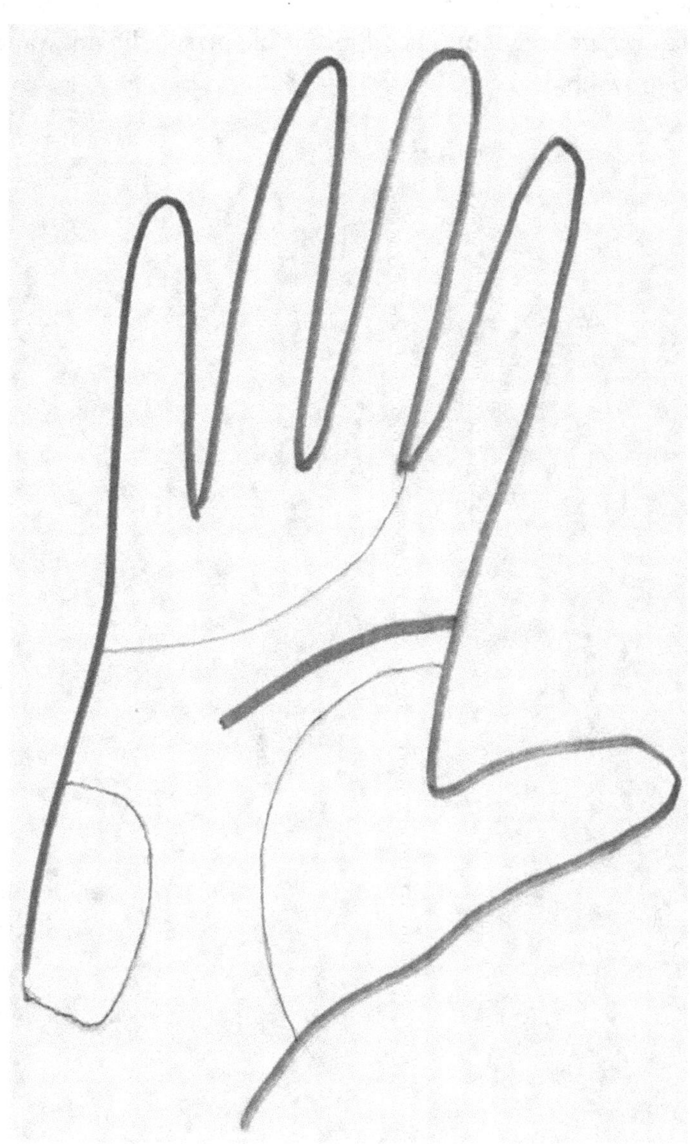

9. Head line tied to the life line at the beginning – Means they will always think about what their family thinks before they go ahead and make a big decision. If tied for more than an average length of time, it means the person did not want to grow up.

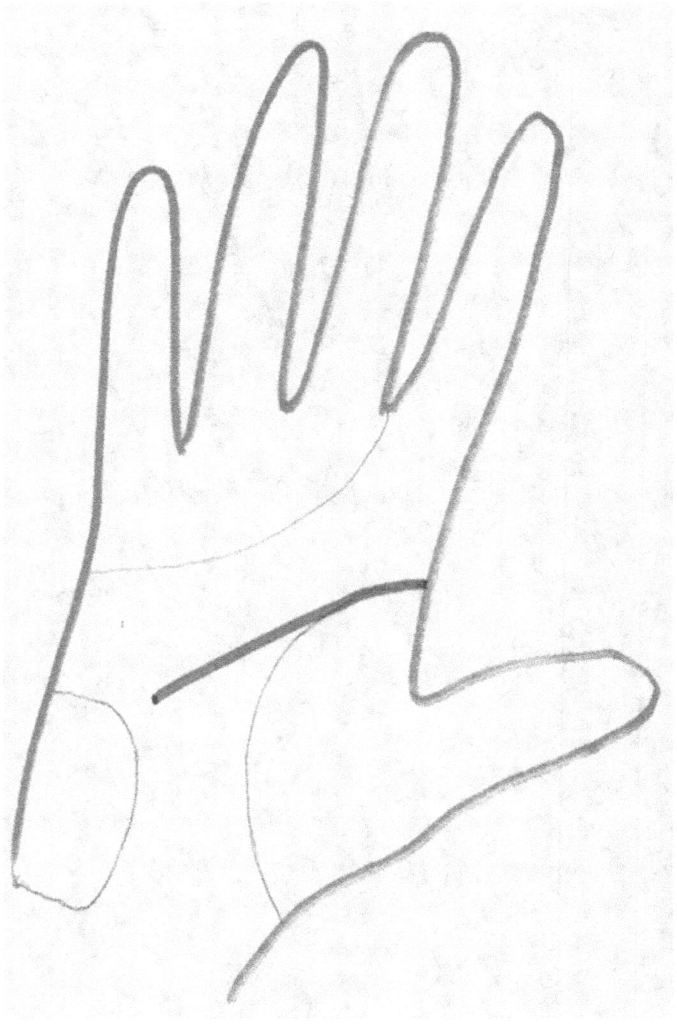

10. Head line that goes straight down to Neptune – Are in direct contact with their subconscious mind; it is very rare. I have seen this line on a lady who had epilepsy.

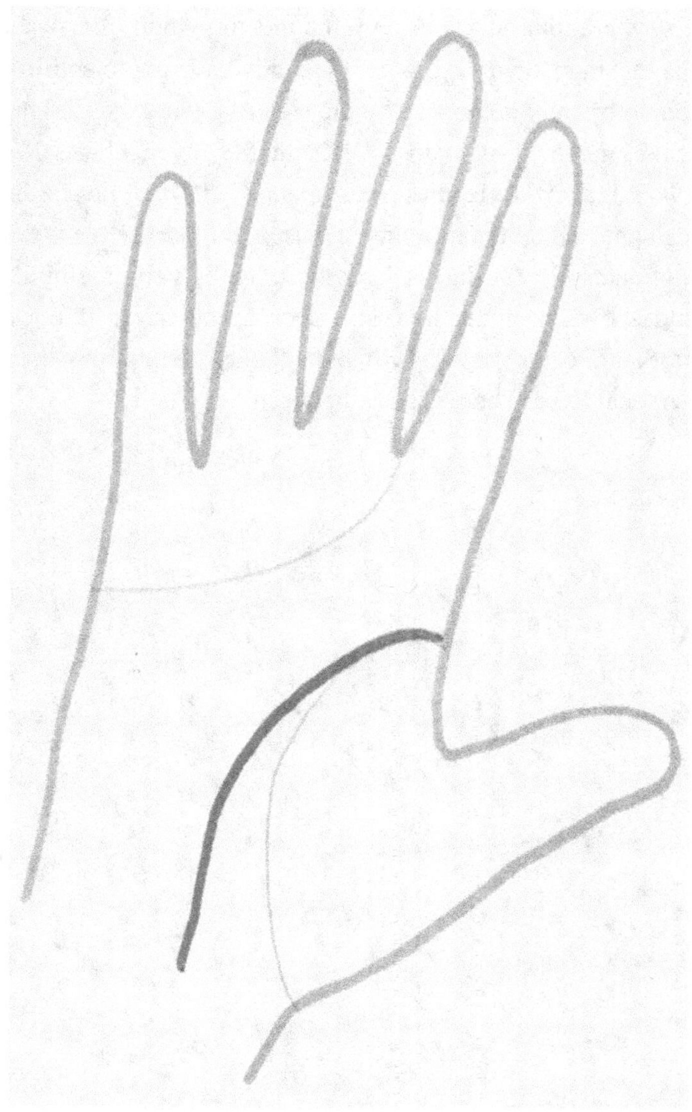

11. A simian head line – A simian head line is when the heart and head line appear as just one line. It means the person cannot separate their thoughts from their feelings, so, with every thought comes a feeling. I have read elsewhere that it is a sign the doctors look for when diagnosing Down syndrome. I recently have got to confirm this to be true. It can also be the sign of a workaholic. This makes me think of Andrew O'Keeth, the guy that hosts *The Chase Australia*. He has the simian line in both hands; he also appears on the morning shows, and I hear he reads the dictionary for fun in his spare time. He is very intelligent and shows a simian line isn't such a bad thing. If not a workaholic the person will put all their effort into their personal lives. There is no in between.

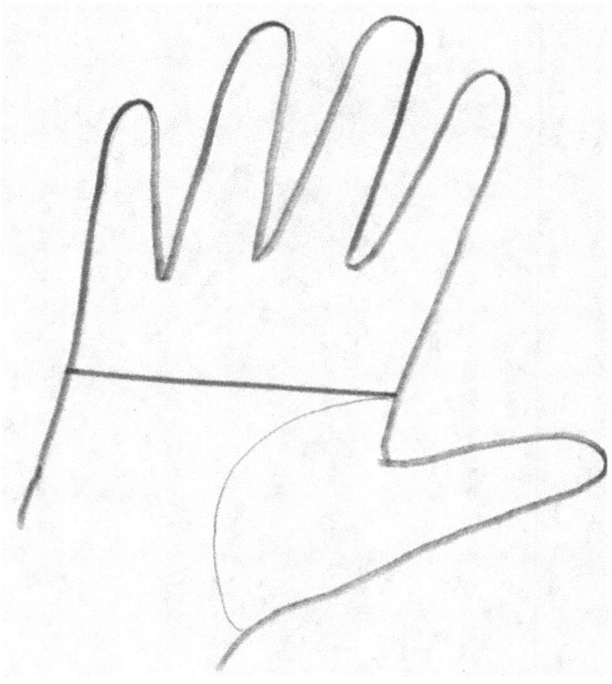

A writer's fork on the end of the head line – Means the person has a talent for writing. Check both hands. They will use their writing to fill out paperwork as part of their job, but if only on the passive hand will use it for more personal reasons and are more likely to publish. In this case check for a royalties mark found on page 110.

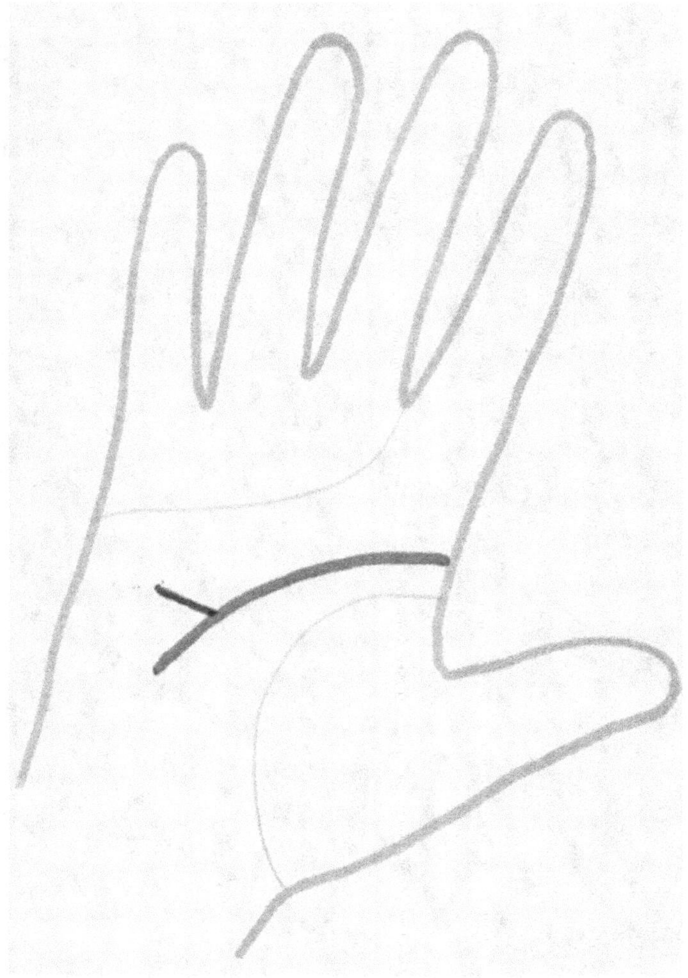

A cross inside a square on the head line – Means a full recovery from a head injury.

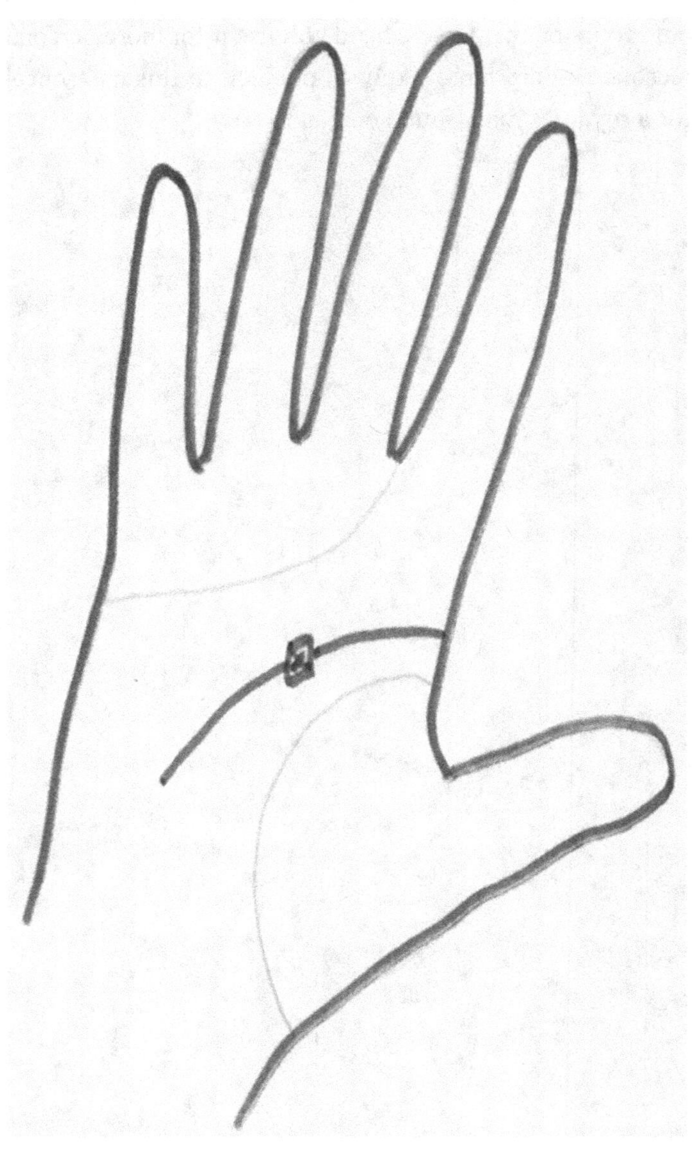

A chained head line – The person gets a lot of headaches or migraines.

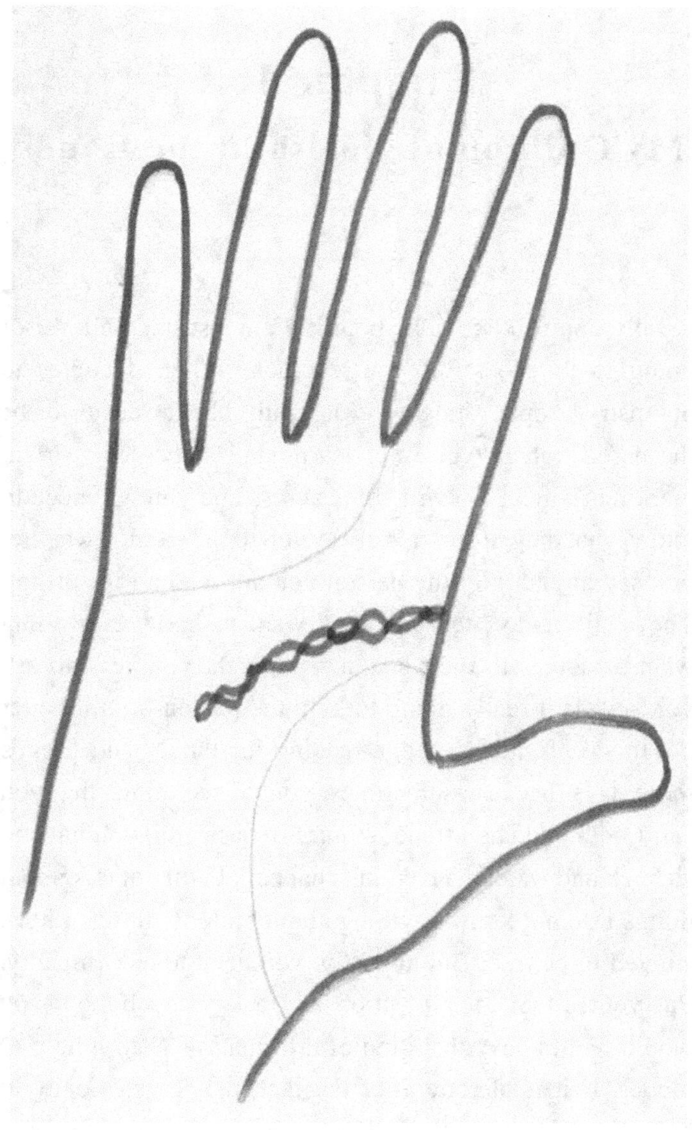

Chapter 16
My Opinion of Health in the Hands

I really don't like to talk about it. I am a strong believer of going to the doctor if you're crook. When it comes to palmistry, some things to do with health need to be discussed when you are learning. There are certain markings which you will come across and you will need to know what they mean. It is always up to the palmist whether you say anything to the person you are reading for or not. They will always tell you they want to know everything when it comes to their health. Although, you need to ask yourself, is it really going to help the person or is it better not to say. I know I dodge reading for family and friends these days, because sometimes, you do see things that you can't do a goddamn thing about. So, basically, you have to sit back and watch when things happen. I will not talk about things I do not know anything about but only things I have studied to be true. But honestly, you need to use empathy. Put yourself in their position and ask yourself how you would feel to have that kind of information. Will it help or hinder. If it is already after the fact, it is always okay to mention. If it is something they can avoid by knowing about it, fine. Otherwise, keep it to yourself.

The reason I am so strict about these things is I was told, years ago, by a palmist I met in Bundaberg Australia, that I would die of a heart attack at the age of 49. It has always been in the back of my mind, and I have given up smoking and try to eat healthy and exercise regularly. So as much as I have done to dodge it happening, I won't know whether it is true or not until I am well and truly past that age. It has personally not helped me at all to know this in advance, aside from taking out funeral insurance, just in case. So, as they say, knowledge is power, so use it wisely. Build people up, don't tear them down.

On the subject of health, if there is a traumatic injury to the body, the person often loses all the minor lines on their hands, and they won't return until the body is well and truly recovered.

Chapter 17
Life Line

Does not tell you what age you are going to die.

1. A strong deep life line – Belongs to a physically fit person, no matter what the length is.

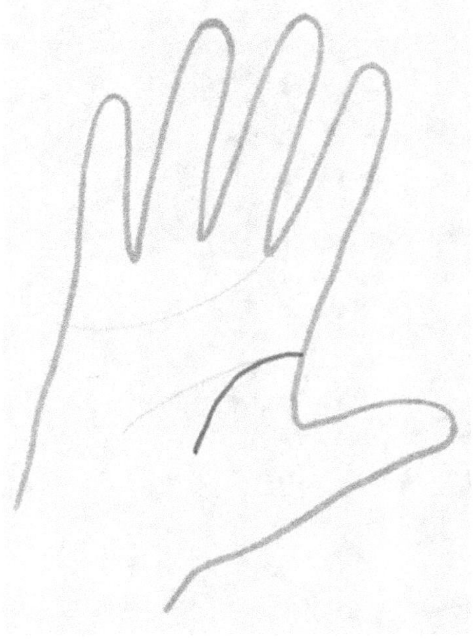

2. A light weak-looking life line – Can show the person does not have much physical energy. If they have a strong head line, this can make up for it a little.

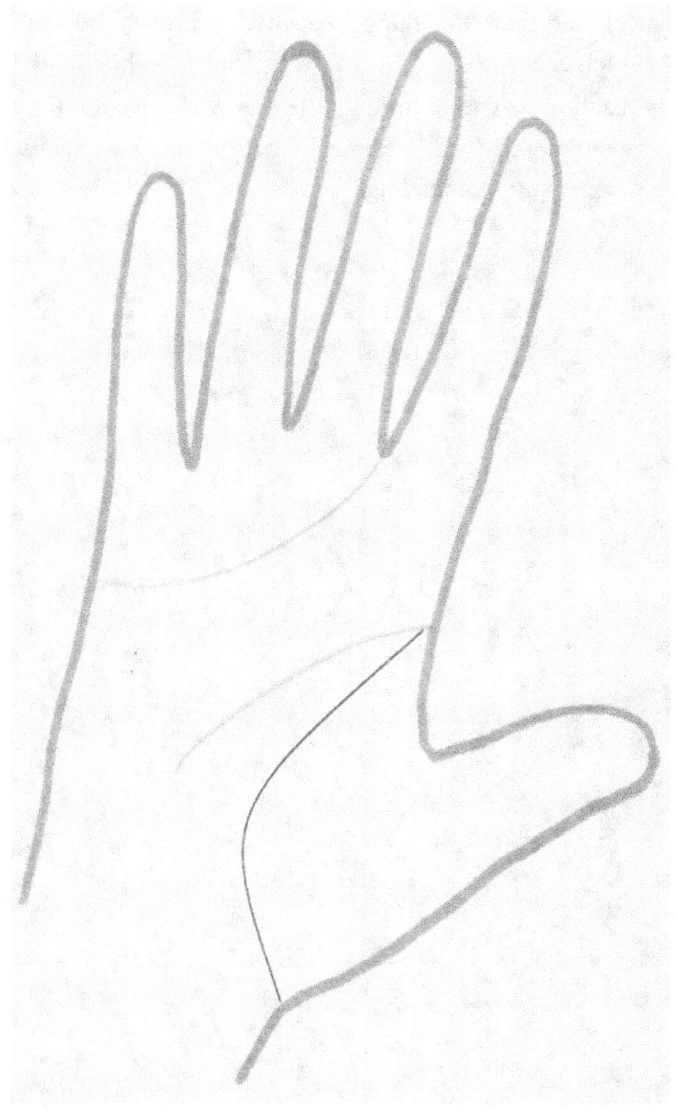

3. If the life line has a break in it then continues – The person will have a sudden lifestyle change for some reason. I remember seeing this guy at a party, years ago, who wanted his palm read. So when I saw this marking on his hand, I said that something happened to him at the age of 22 which caused him to have a huge change in his lifestyle. His reaction was to tell me that it was when he shot a man and went to jail for his crime. It will amaze you at times what comes up in a reading.

4. If the line has an overlapping line – It means the new thing kicks in before the new lifestyle changes.

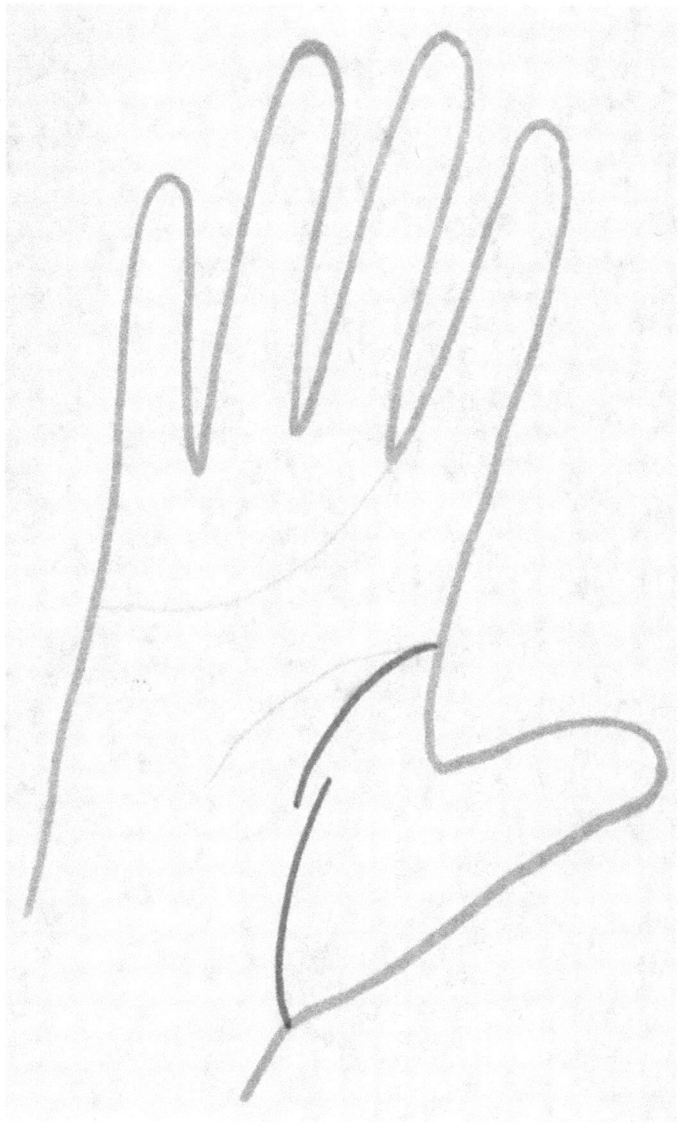

5. When the life line swings out into the middle of the hand – It means they like to make the most of every opportunity in life.

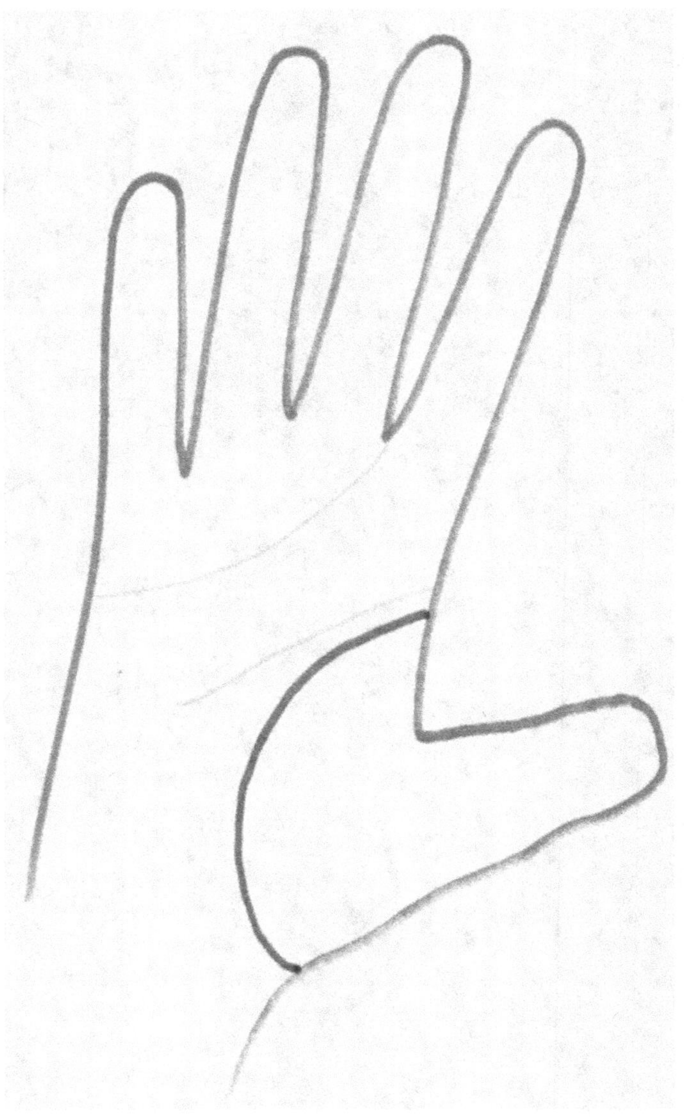

6. An island at the beginning of the life line – Is a sign of
lung problems in the person's childhood.

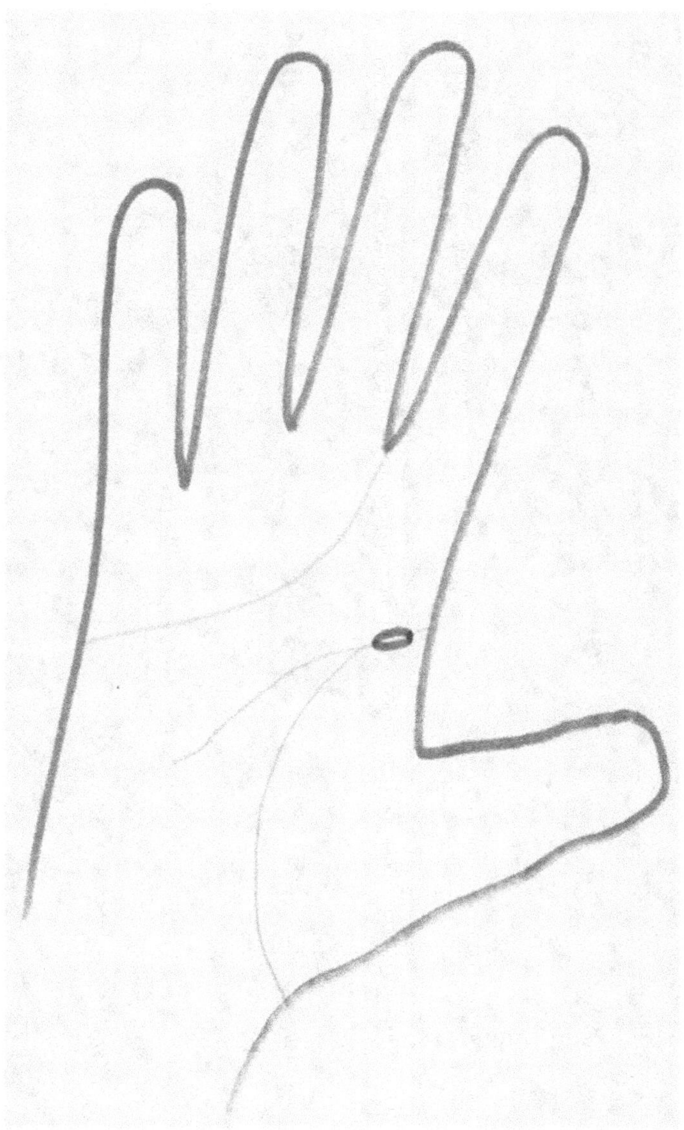

7. If it looks like netting at the beginning – It shows mental illness. Check both hands, they may not show it to the outside world.

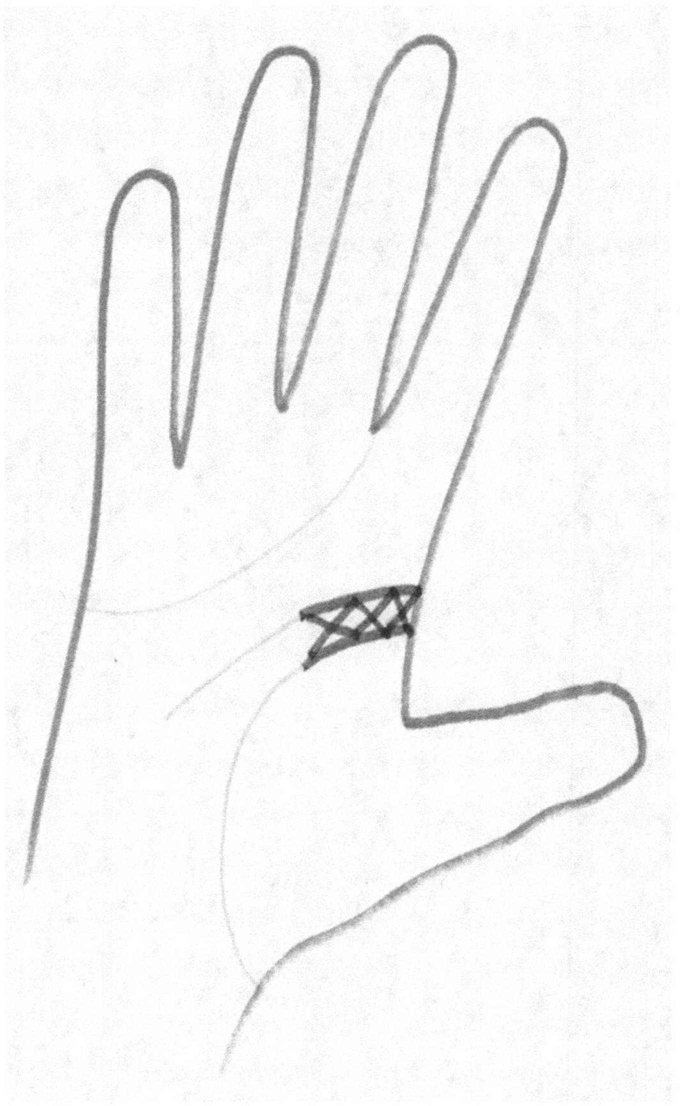

8. An island anywhere on the life line – Means health problems at that time.

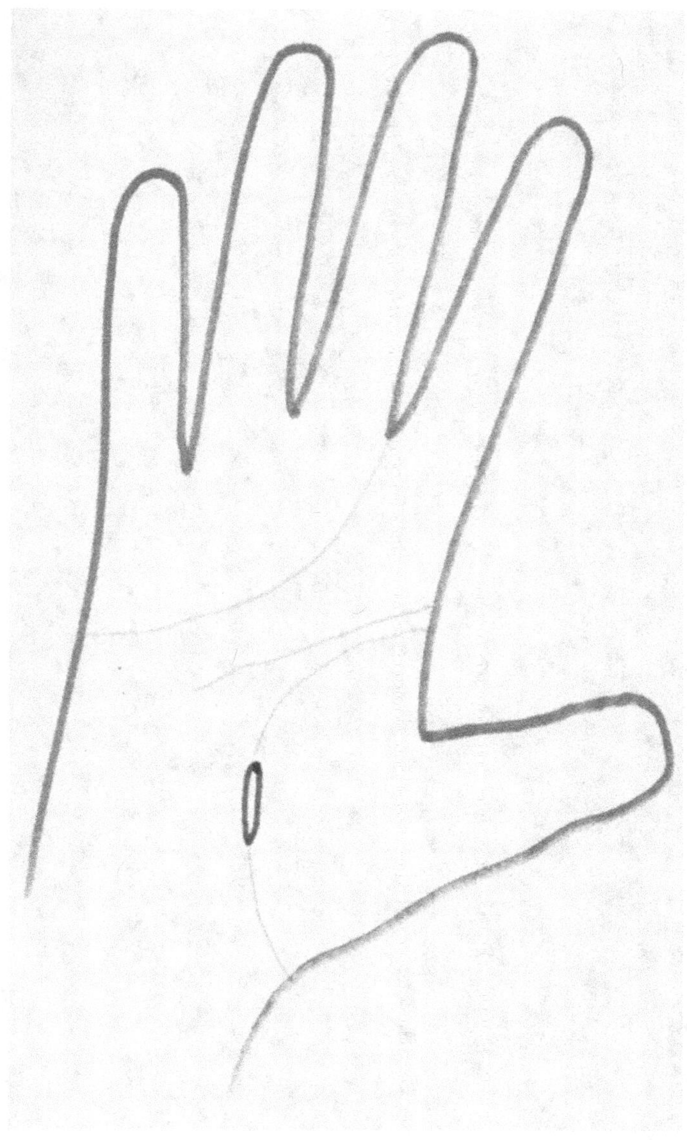

9. When you see little lines going up from the life line –
It is when something or someone has motivated the person to move forward in life.

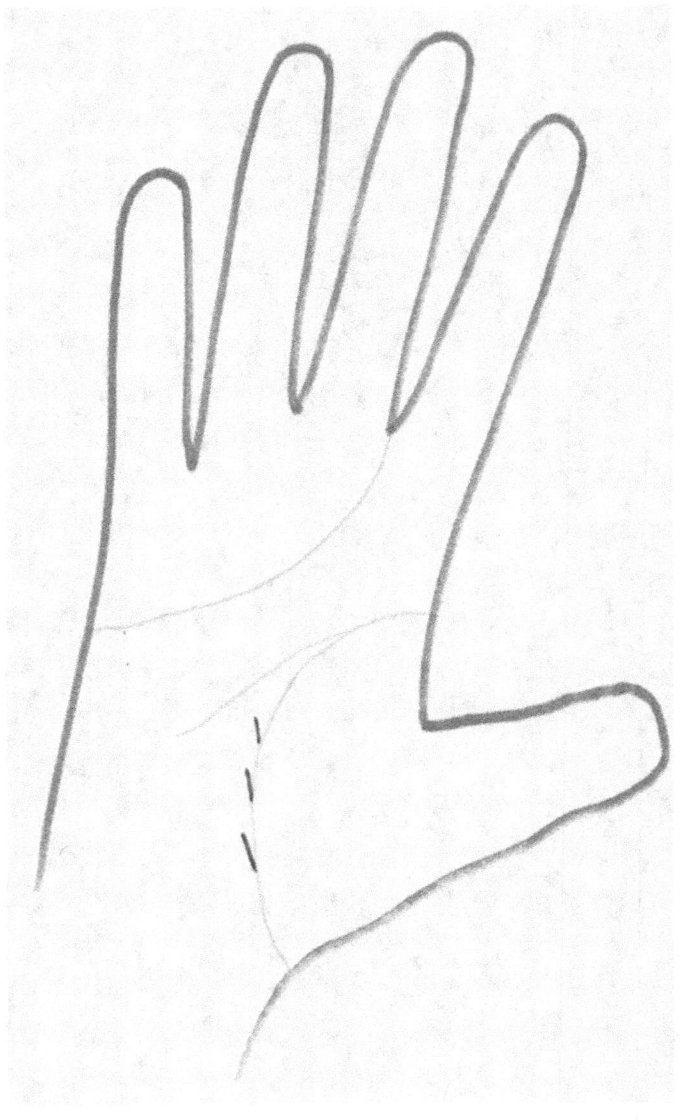

10. Sacrificial marking – Usually seen on the hands of a single parent.

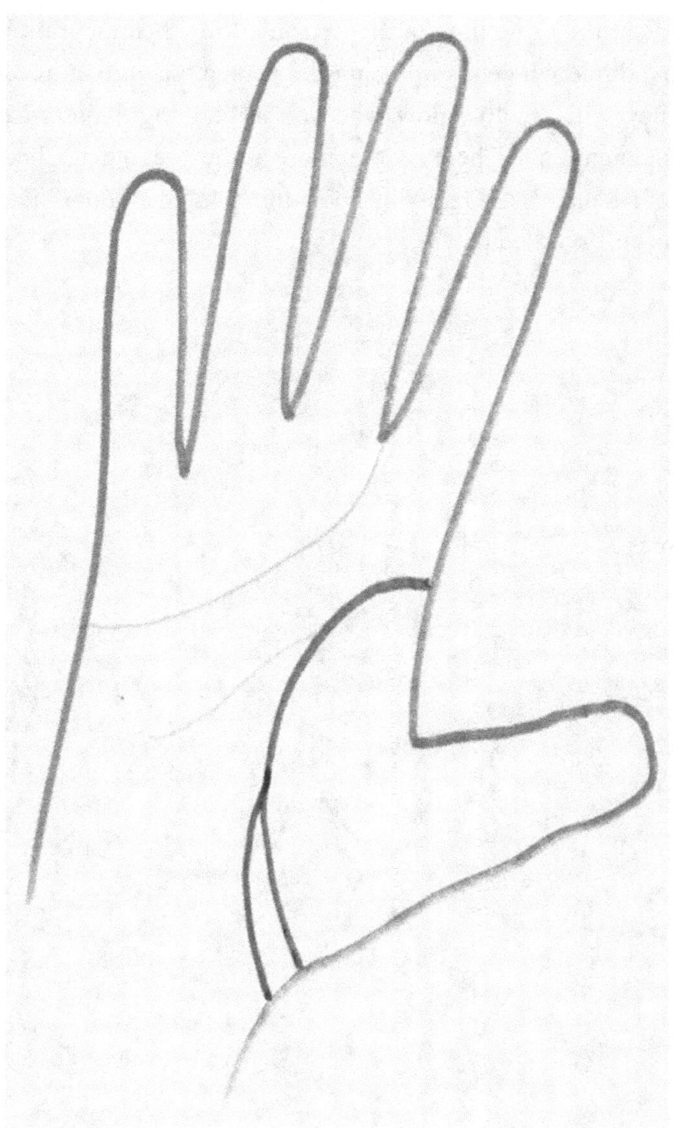

11. Line known as a sister line, inside the life line, running alongside – It means spiritual protection against accident and illness. It usually starts off touching the life line at the same time in the person's life when they lose a loved one who ends up being the person's guardian angel. They will usually know who you are talking about when you mention it. There is often more as they get older. Check both hands. Not really a good thing to mention if they haven't reached that age yet.

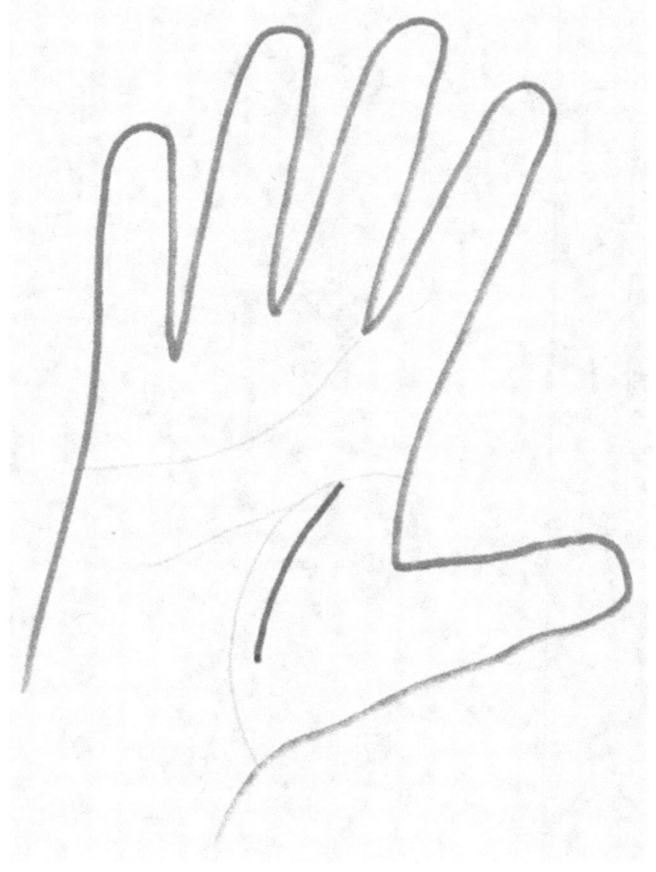

12. If you see a crease that turns upwards, running horizontal inside the life line – The person tends to dwell in the past (a), and if it turns downwards, they like to look forward to the future (b).

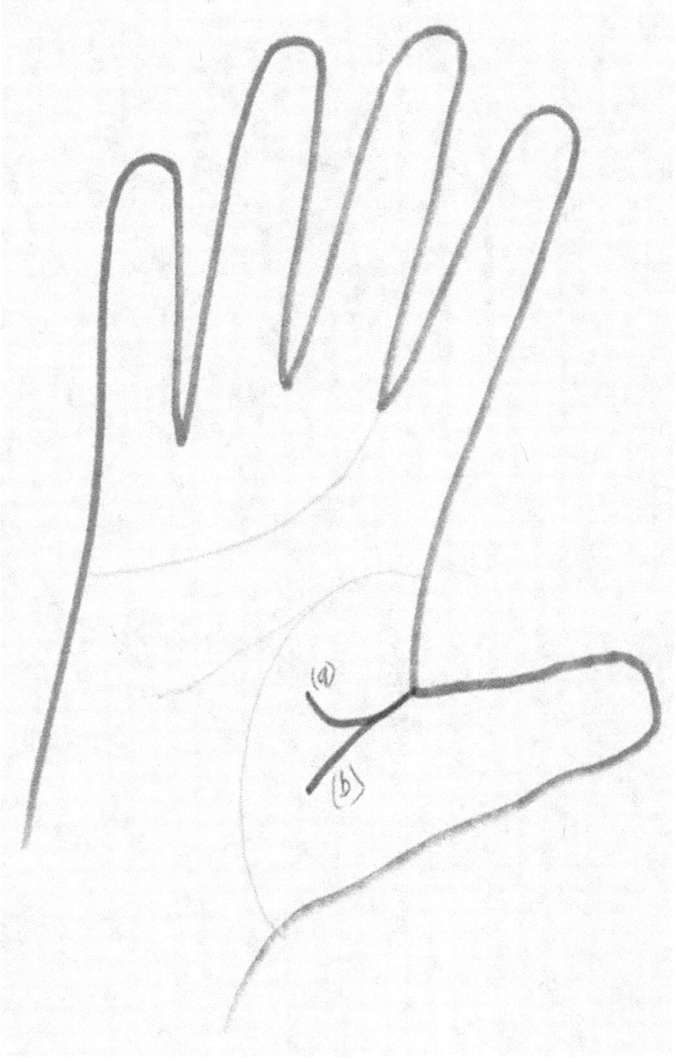

13. If the life line pitters out at the end – The person will be unwell for some time before they die.

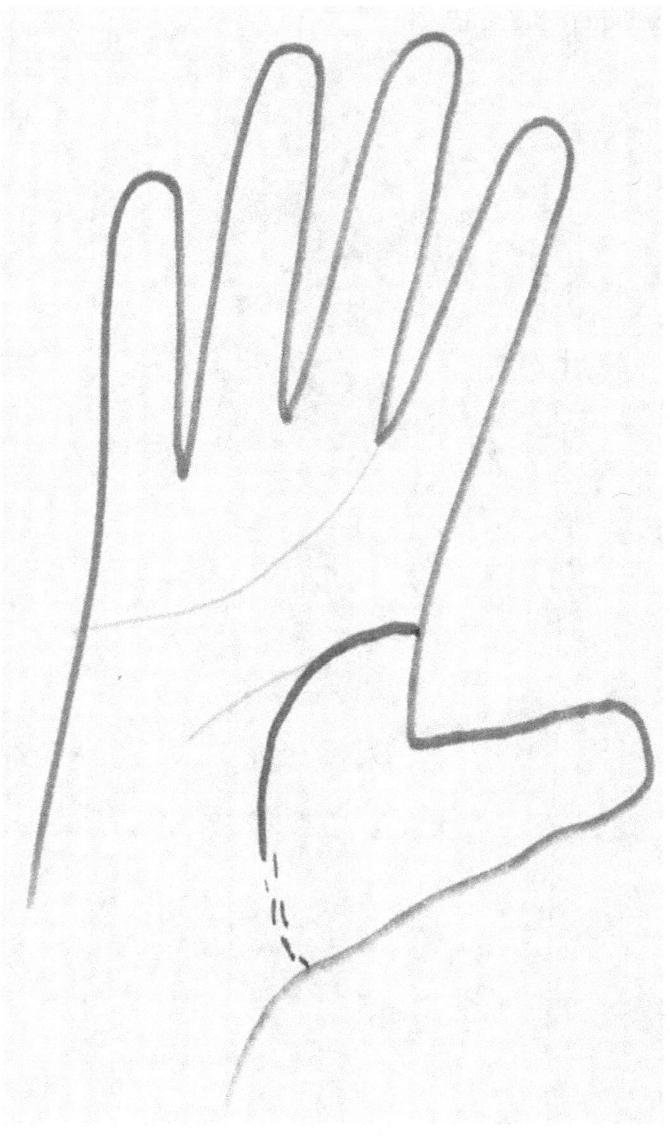

Chapter 18
Fate or Work Line

If the fate line starts low on the palm, it means that the person started work from a really young age.

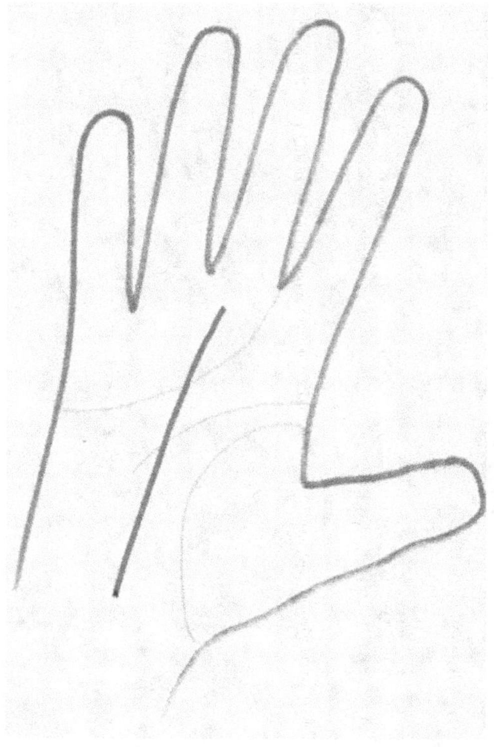

Beginning on the life line – They have received help
from the family with work with their very first job

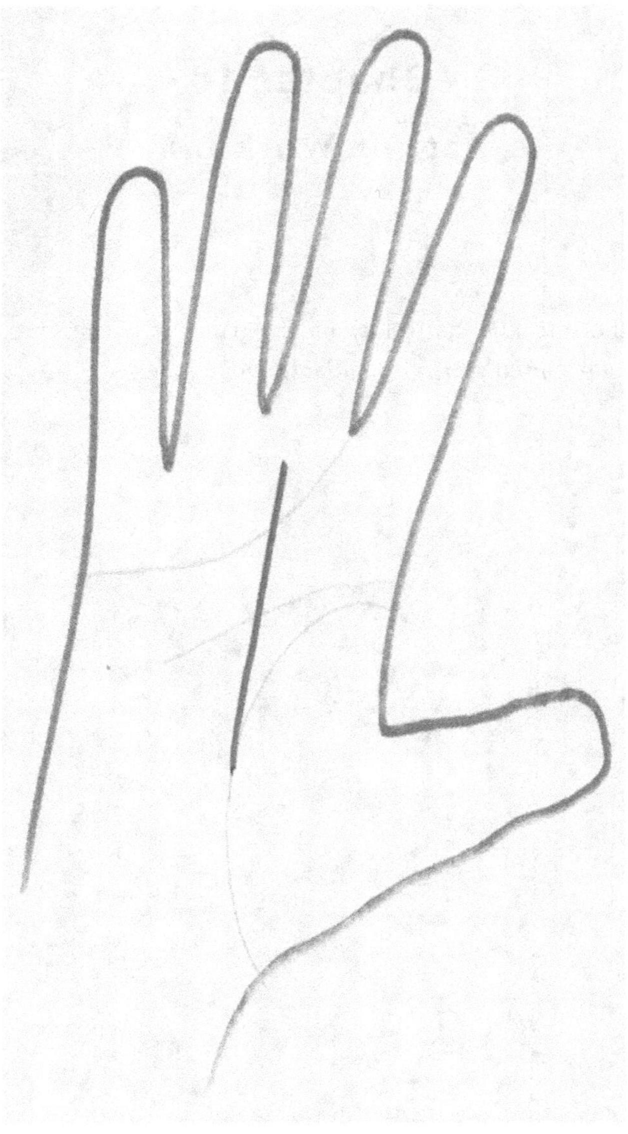

Starting on the Luna mount – Means they got help from outside the family with work.

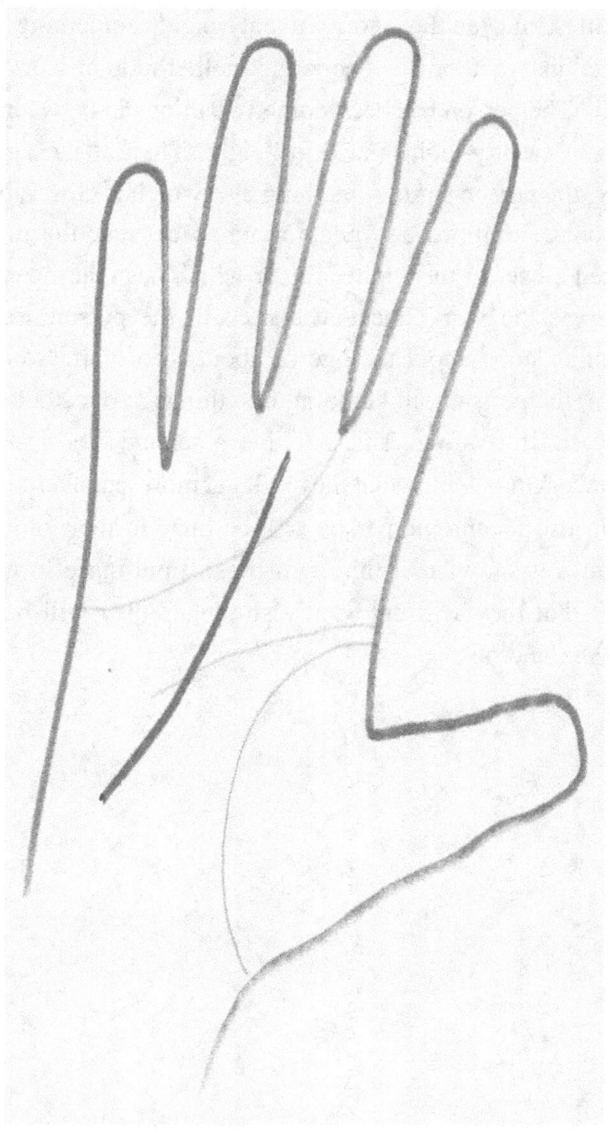

Multiple fate (work) lines – You need to consider the timing on the hand of when certain lines start and finish. So, this line says that the person started work in his early twenties, and at the age of twenty-eight, something else kicked in, whether it be work and motherhood or work and study. The person has been doing two things in between the ages of twenty-eight and thirty-eight. Then at the age of forty, the person starts something else which is closer to his personal ambitions and goals more so because the line is placed closer to the Jupiter finger which has that meaning. Whereas the work line that started in the person's early twenties stops about the age of about forty-four. So once again, the person will be doing two things at once between forty and forty-four. This is either a second job or study, then working, doing what they will get more satisfaction out of. It also means the person will be busy in their old age, because it shows that they will be still putting effort into work that they will enjoy. It also means they will be too busy to be crook.

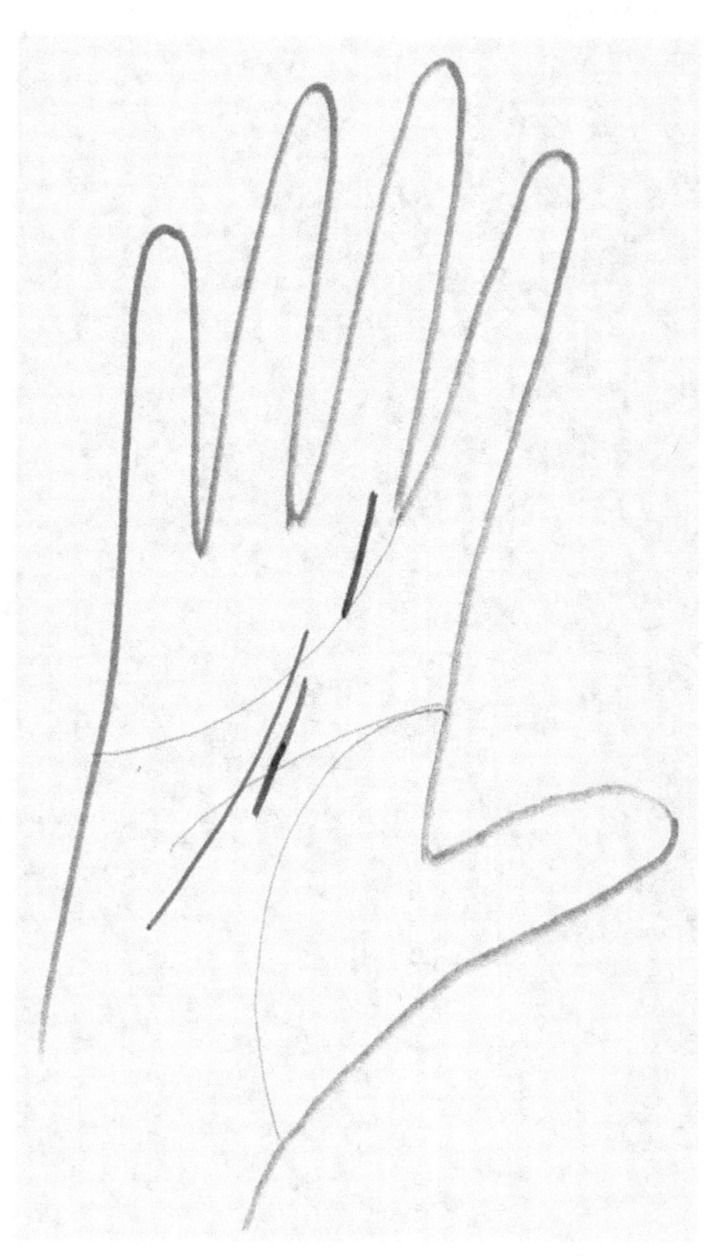

Starting with a fork – Is the sign of a business partnership.

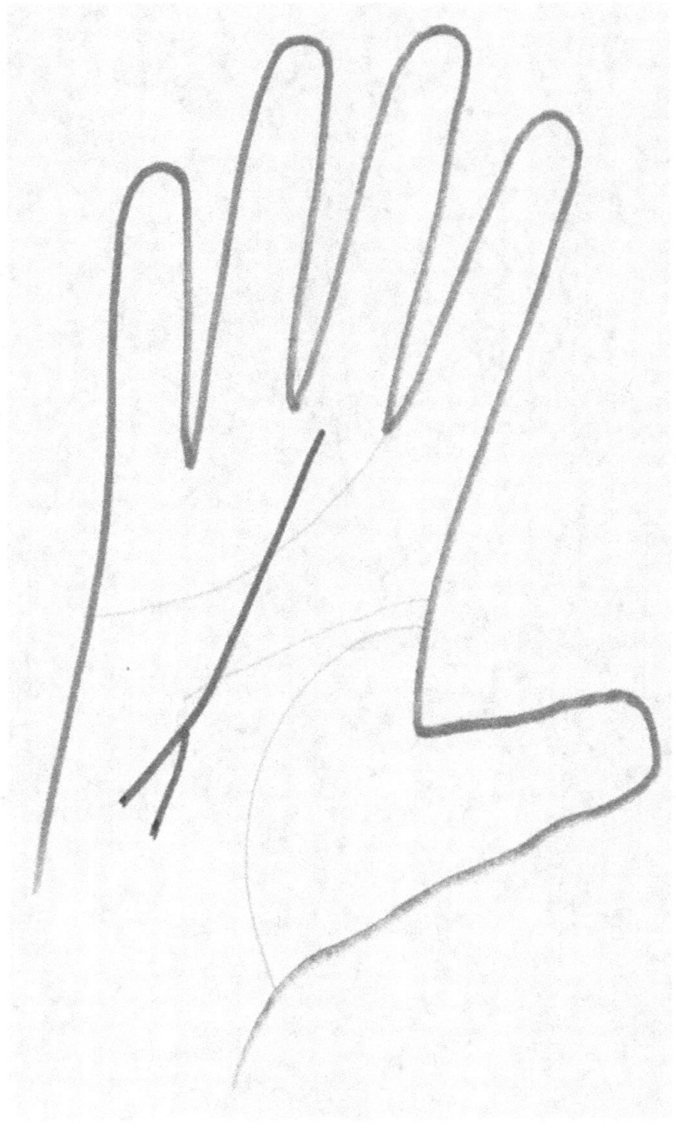

Overseas line connecting to the fate line – Shows some sort of overseas connection to the person. For example they may have been born overseas etc.

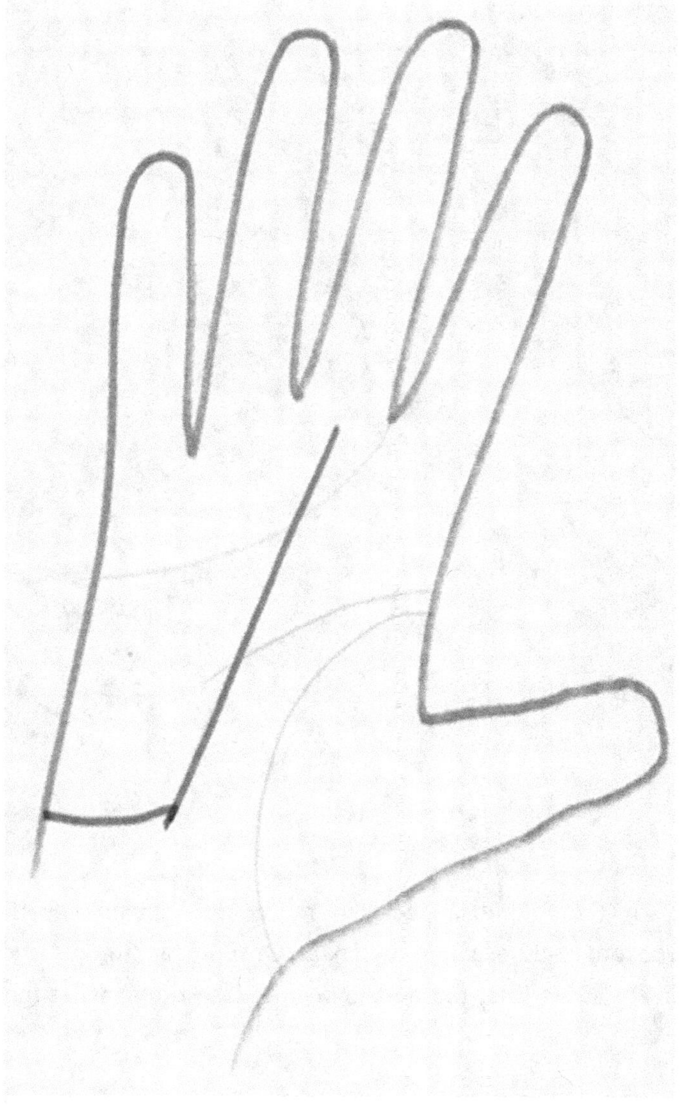

Working from home marking

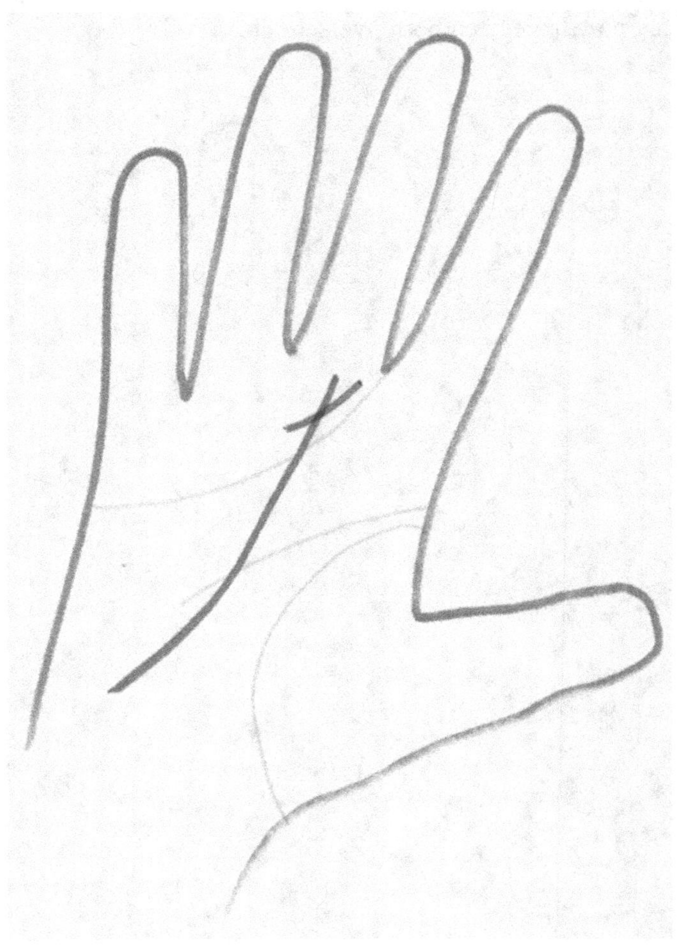

If the fate disappears, it means the person has the freedom to choose their own path. Or if the fate line finishes on the heart line, the person will end up doing what they love.

Chapter 19
Line of the Sun

Line of the sun – Found underneath the Apollo or ring finger, this shows how much happiness and success the person has. Sometimes the person will have a few lines in this area, and the more of and the deeper and darker they are, the more happiness and success the person will have. Check both hands, they might feel it more than it shows to the outside world.

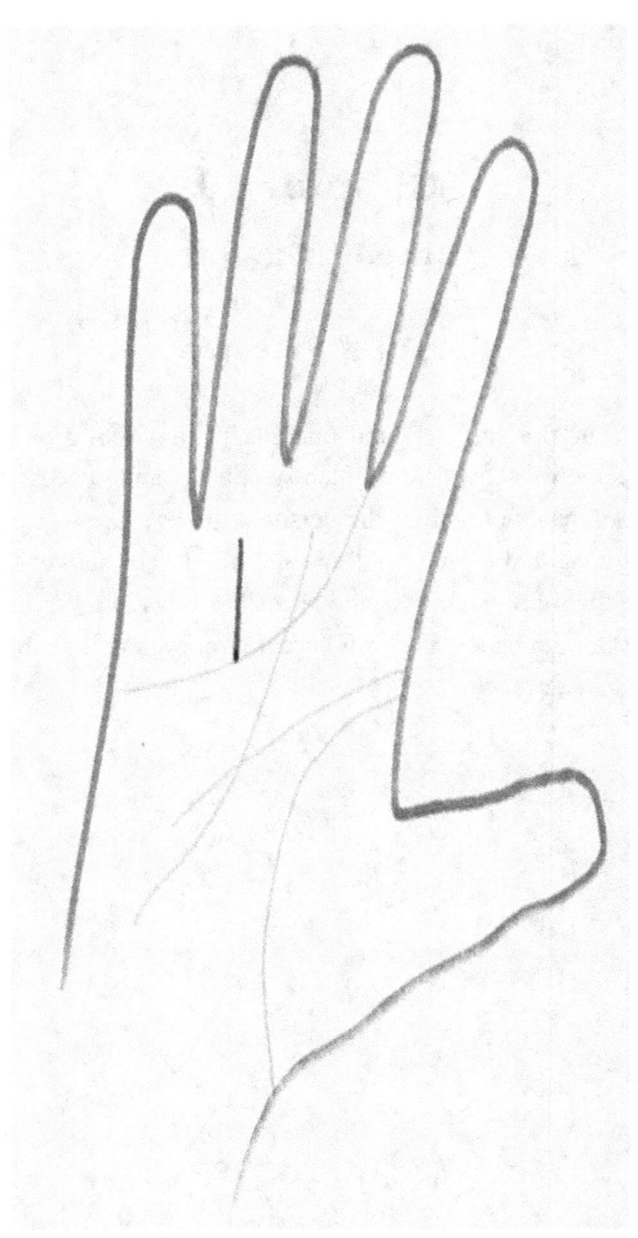

How pessimistic thinking can put a cloud over the finger of the sun in palmistry terms, so you are not feeling the happiness and success that they do show as having by the presence of the line of the sun. It can be worked on just by not being so pessimistic with your thinking. Try to catch yourself out when you know that you are, and sing a little song or listen to your breathing or something just to change your headspace.

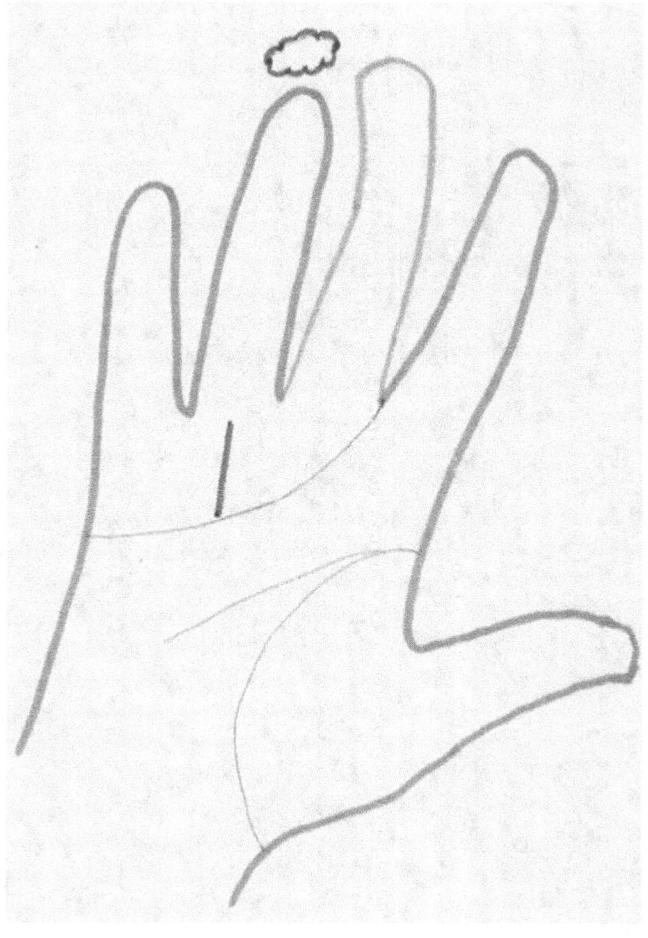

A line coming from the head line to the line of the sun – Means the person will make money from an idea they have had.

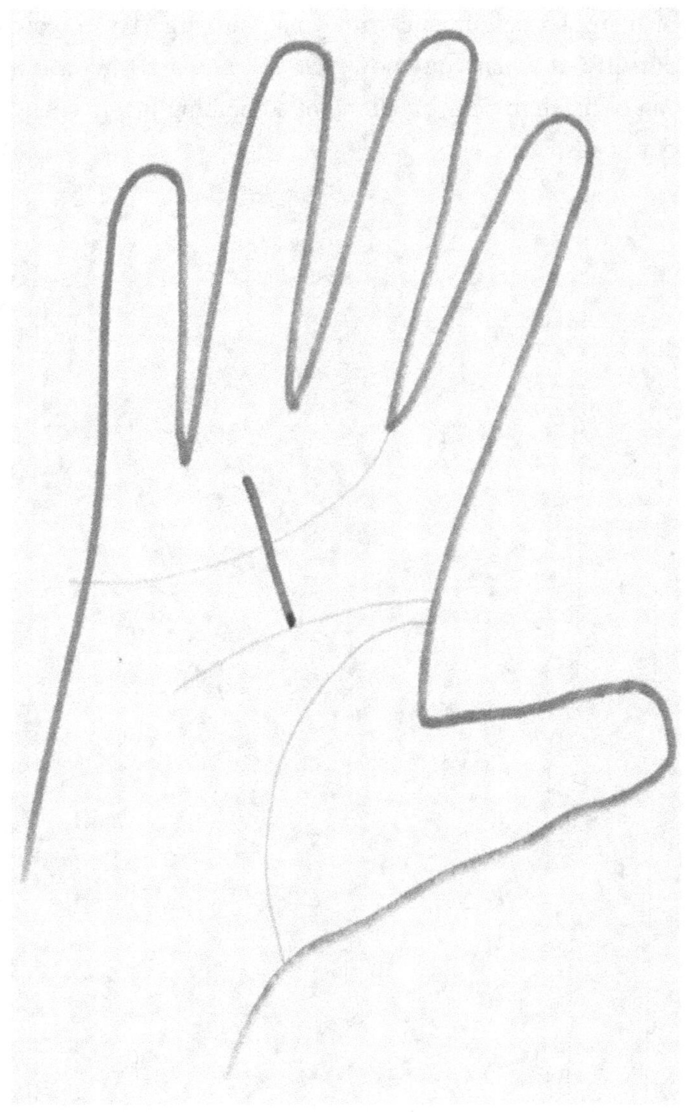

**If there are lines running up towards the line of the
sun in a diagonal direction** – Each one stands for a lump
sum of money the person will get, such as superannuation
or inheritance, or even a lotto win.

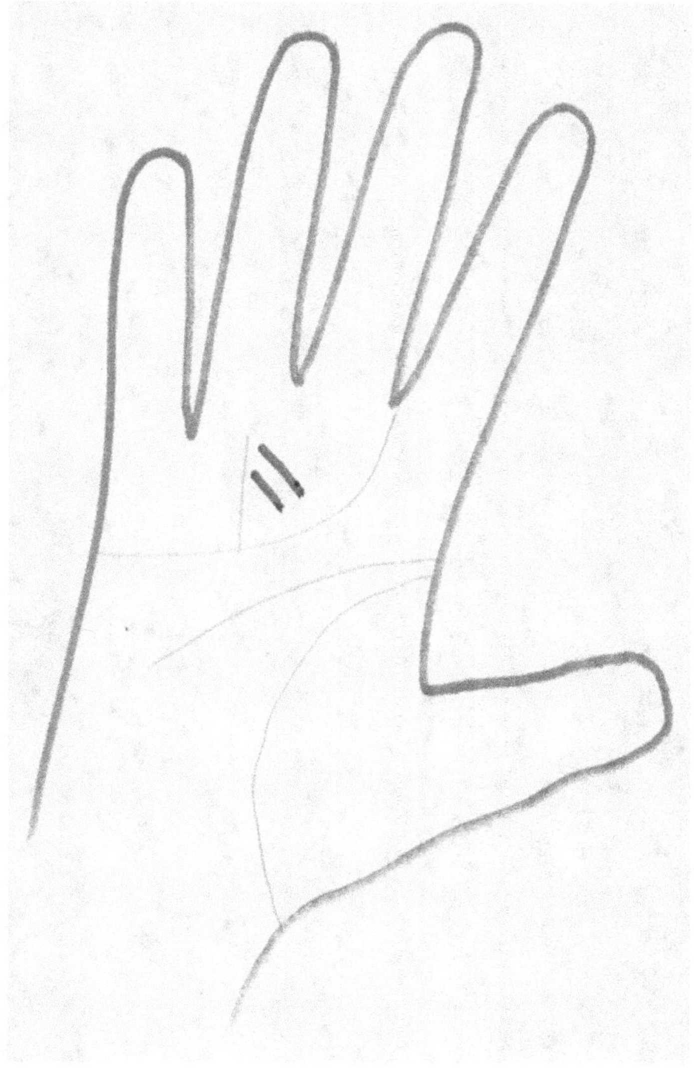

If there is a star on the mount of Apollo – It means the person will earn money from royalties.

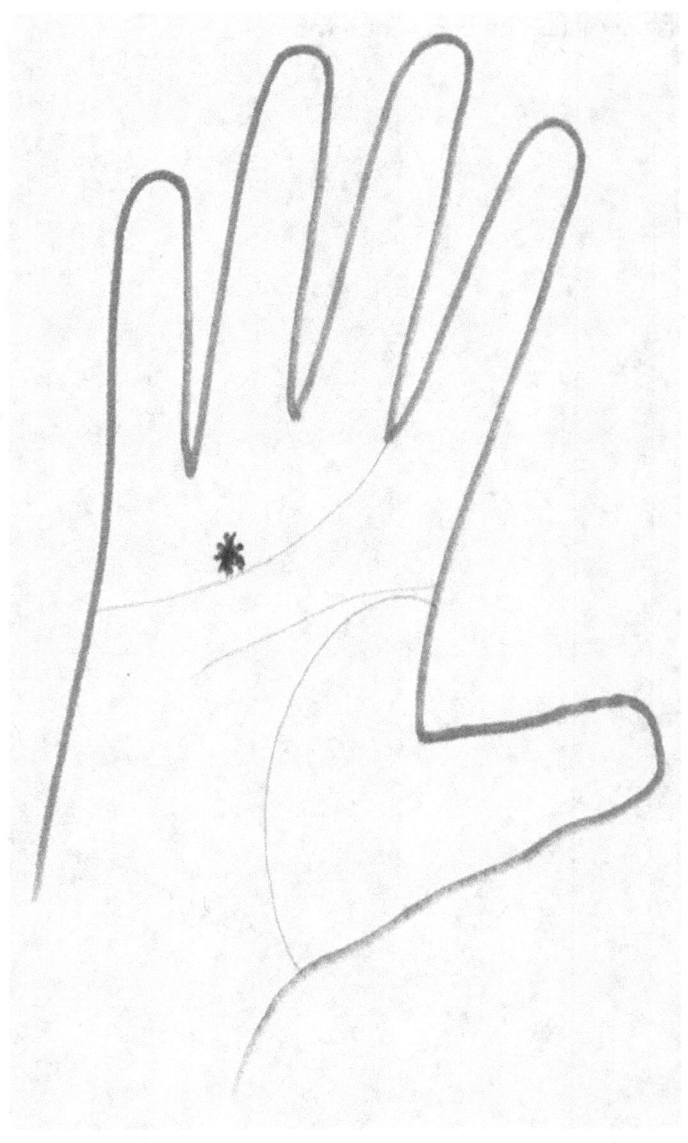

A line that goes from the heart line to the Apollo mount – It means the person gains money through marriage or from a divorce.

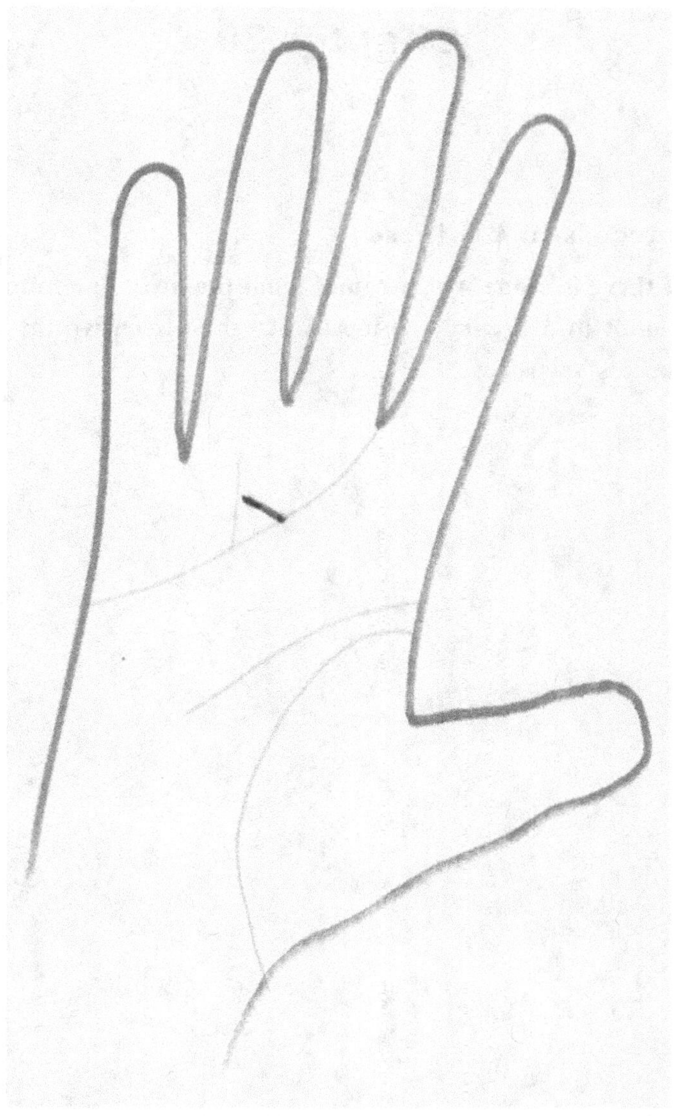

Chapter 20

Success in Business

If there is a line which comes from the head line to the mount of Mercury – It means that the person will have success in business.

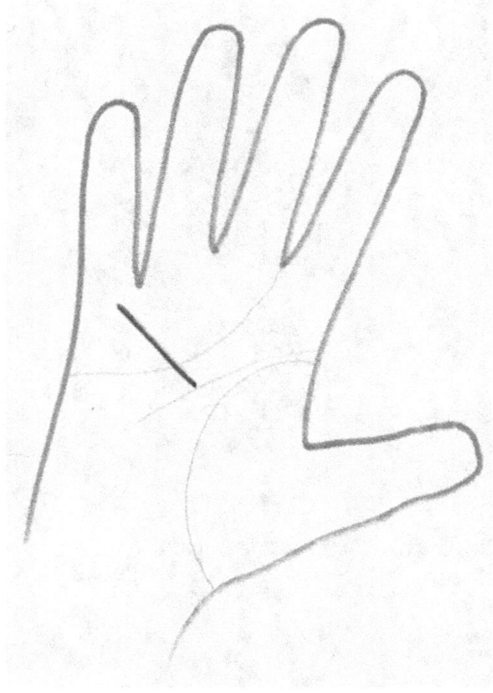

The Health Line or Line of Intuition

It means the person has an interest in the subject of health and always will. It also shows how intuitive the person can be; the strength and quality will show just how much.

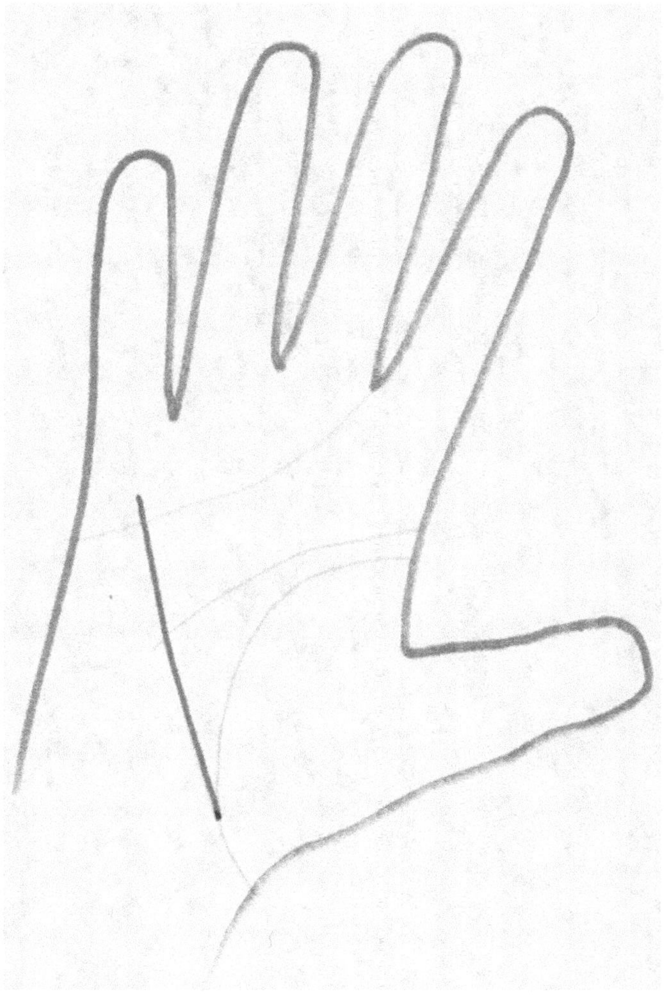

If a line runs from the health line up to the Apollo mount – It means that is the age the person started to work in the health industry. (In this case it would be at age thirty-seven years old.)

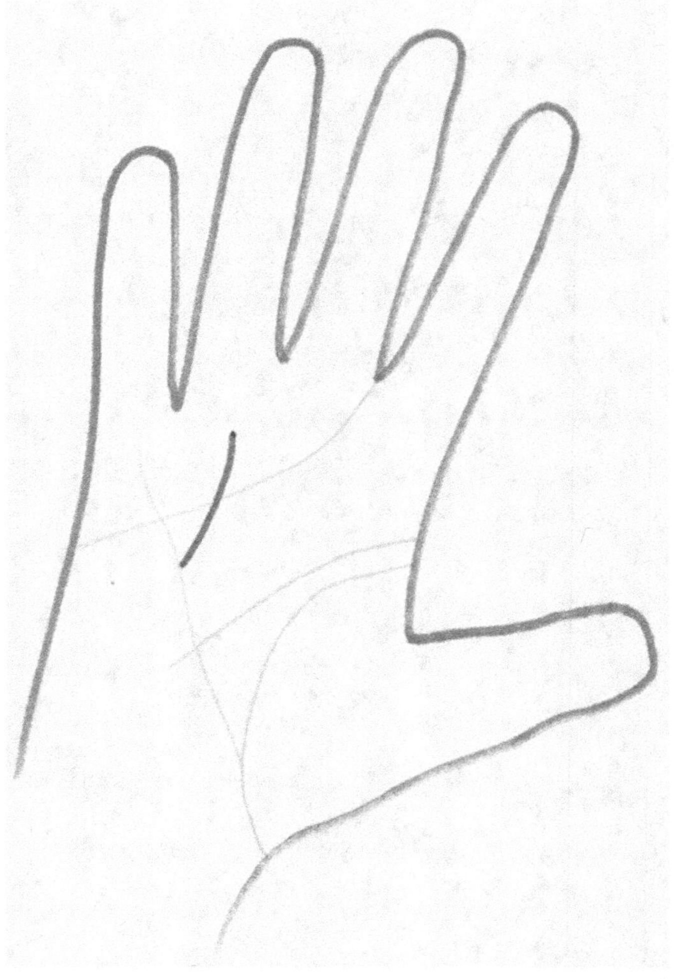

Chapter 21

Travel Lines

Overseas and interstate, depending on the length and timing from the base upwards on the edge of the Luna mount. Overseas are the longer ones and the shorter ones are interstate. Also if you have an overseas line and another one follows that same line it means they go overseas and somewhere else while they are over there.

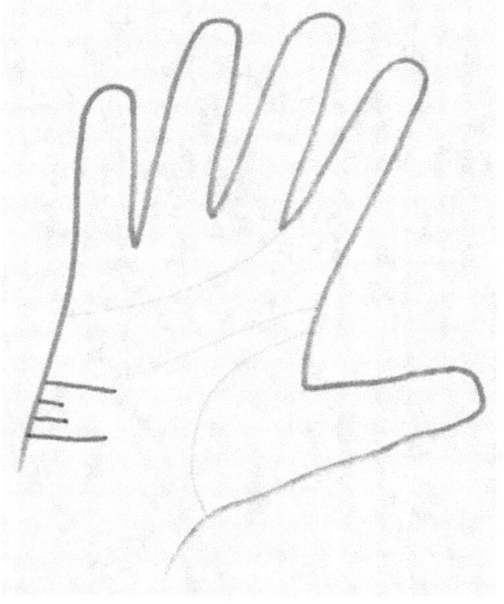

When a travel line turns upward – It is a trip which is to the person's advantage in some way.

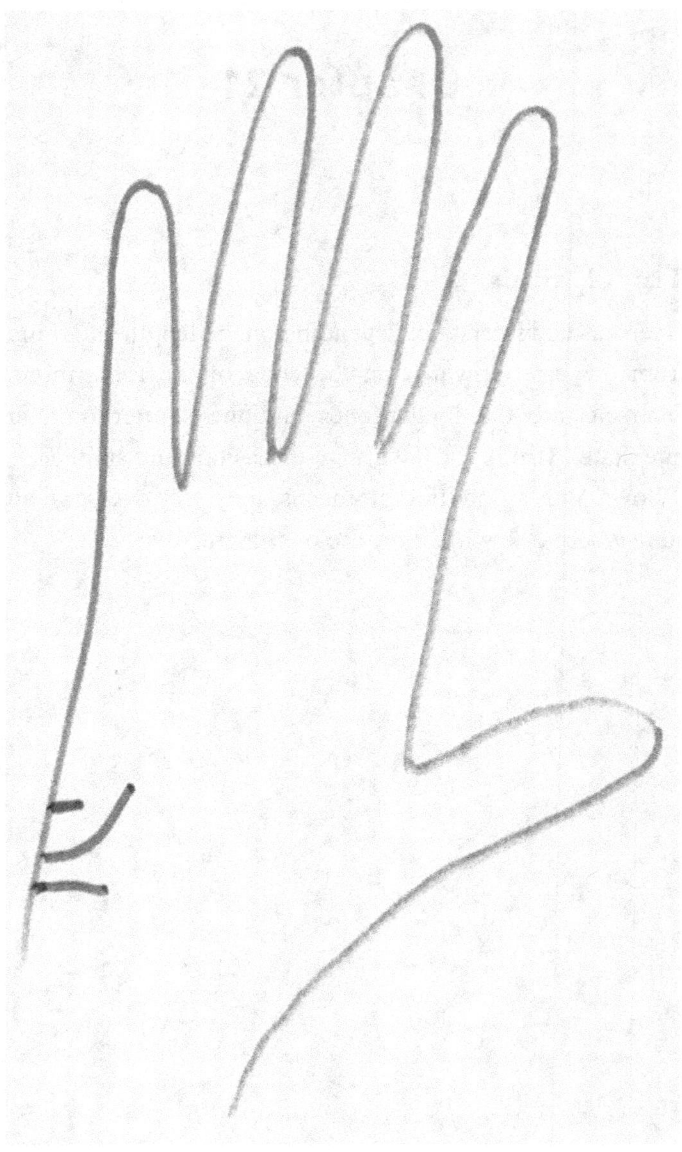

Cruise

A clear cross on the Luna mount – Stands for a cruise.

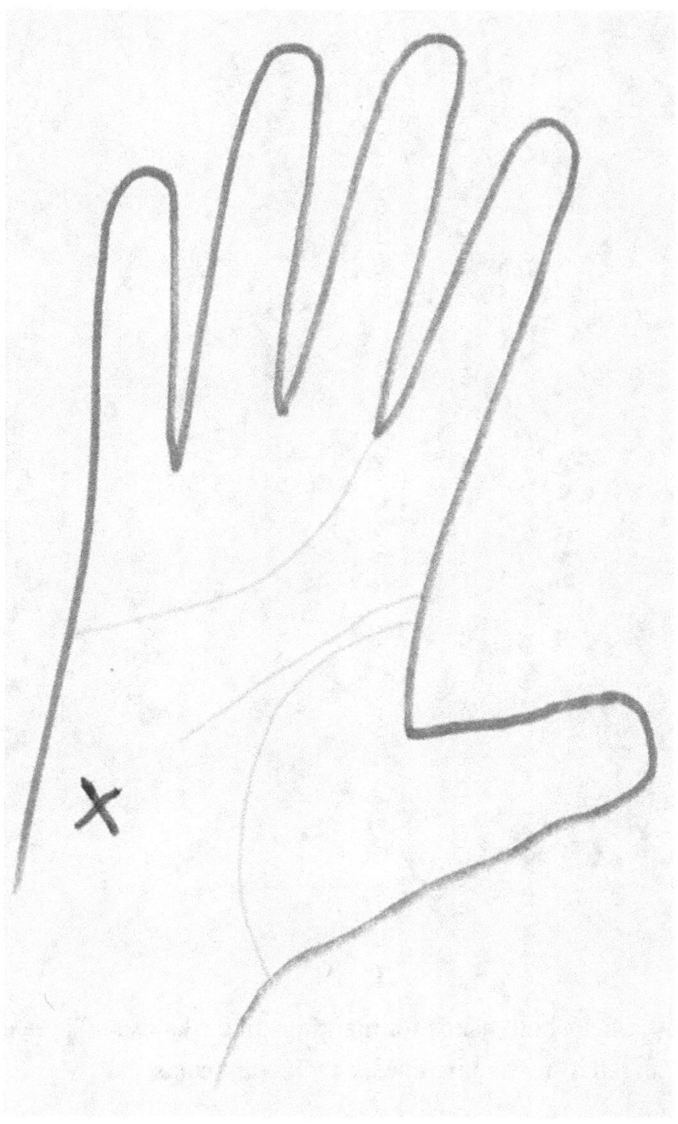

Raclettes

Raclette's are the lines at the wrists. They cover 25 years each.

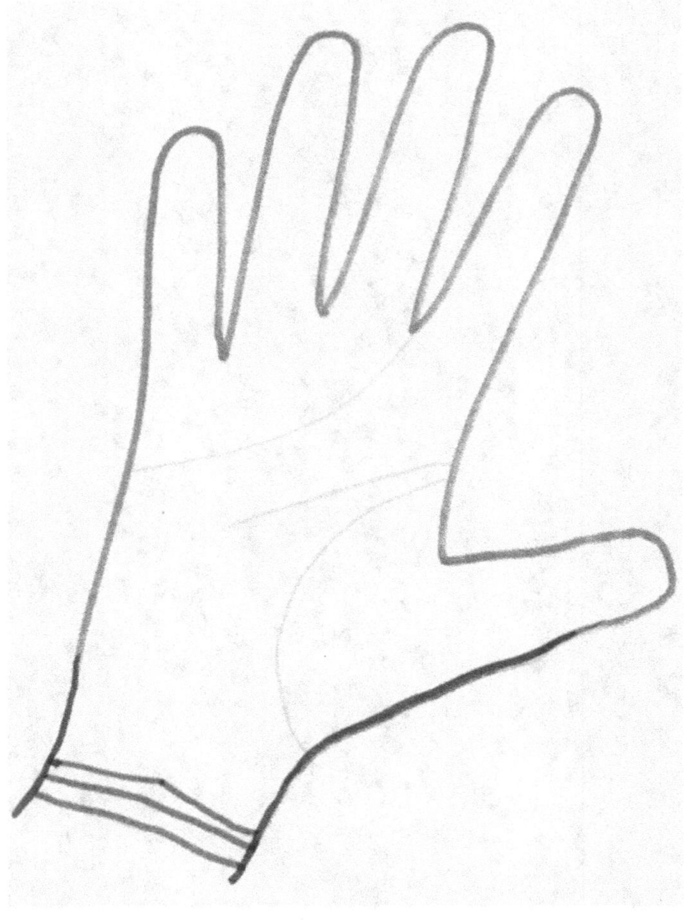

Check both hands for markings like islands and breaks. Can tell a story sometimes, check both hands.

Rings of Solomon

I like to call them rings of wisdom. It means the person is good at understanding other people and giving them really good advice from the other person's point of view. You would expect to find them on a councillor's hands.

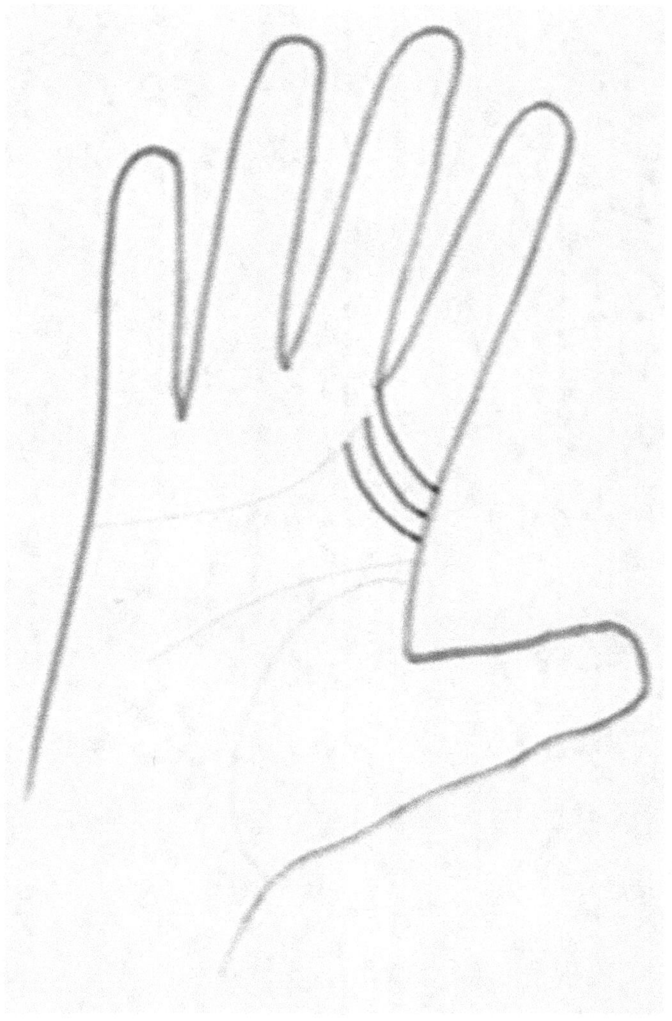

Teacher's Square

The teacher's square – Means the person is good at teaching others.

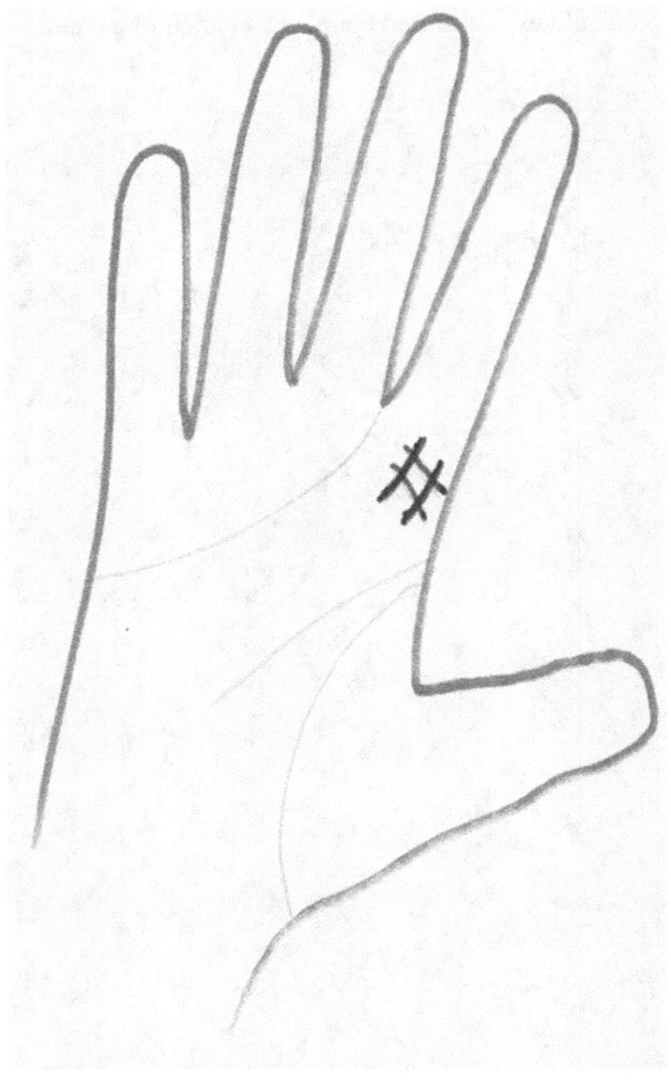

Sibling Lines

Shows how many brothers and sisters the person has. Sometimes it only shows the ones that have some effect on the person's lives. I usually say that you could have ten brothers and sisters for all I know, but there is only two that show up in your hand. If I see two lines there, that is.

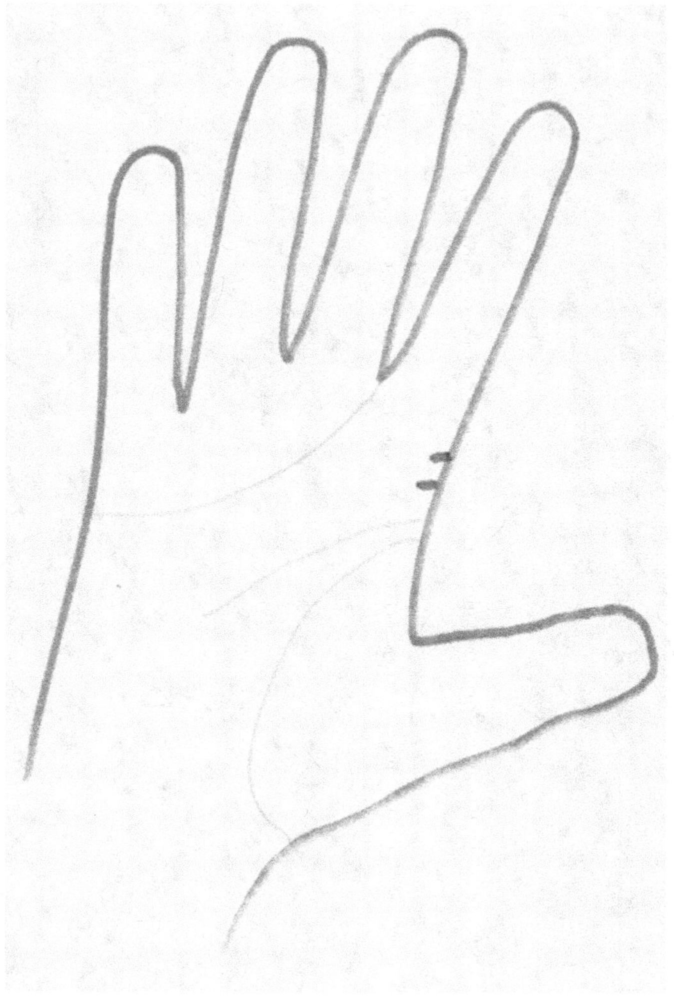

The Money-Maker Line

Means the person has always been good at making a dollar. If there is more than one line in this area, each one stands for a course the person can pass and do well with.

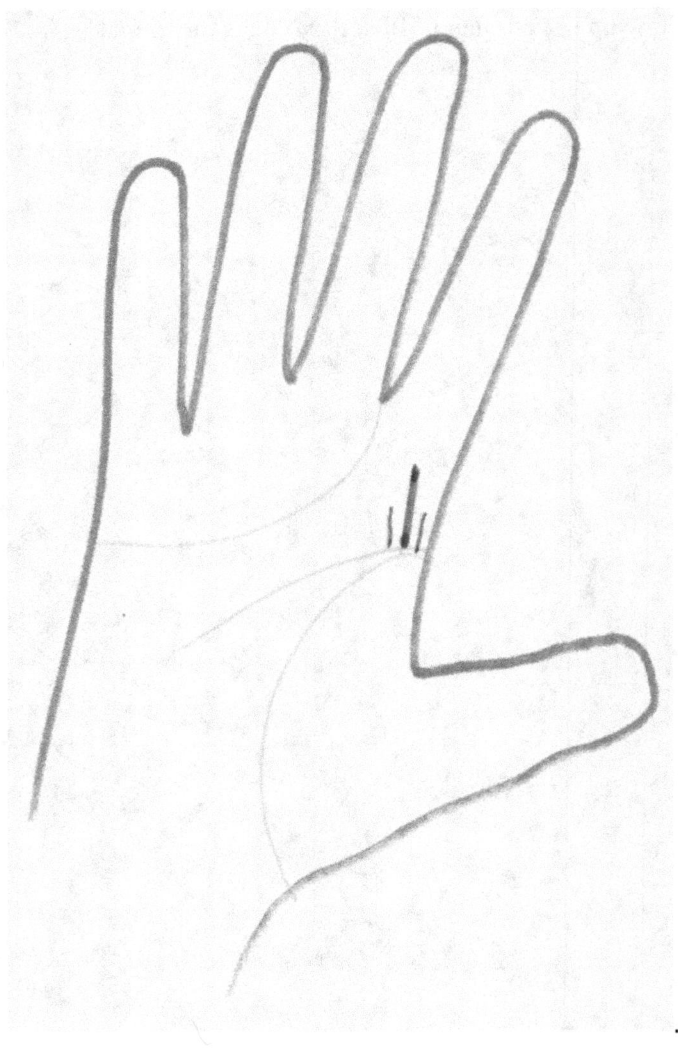

Poison Line

If the poison line is present, the person may have trouble with addiction.

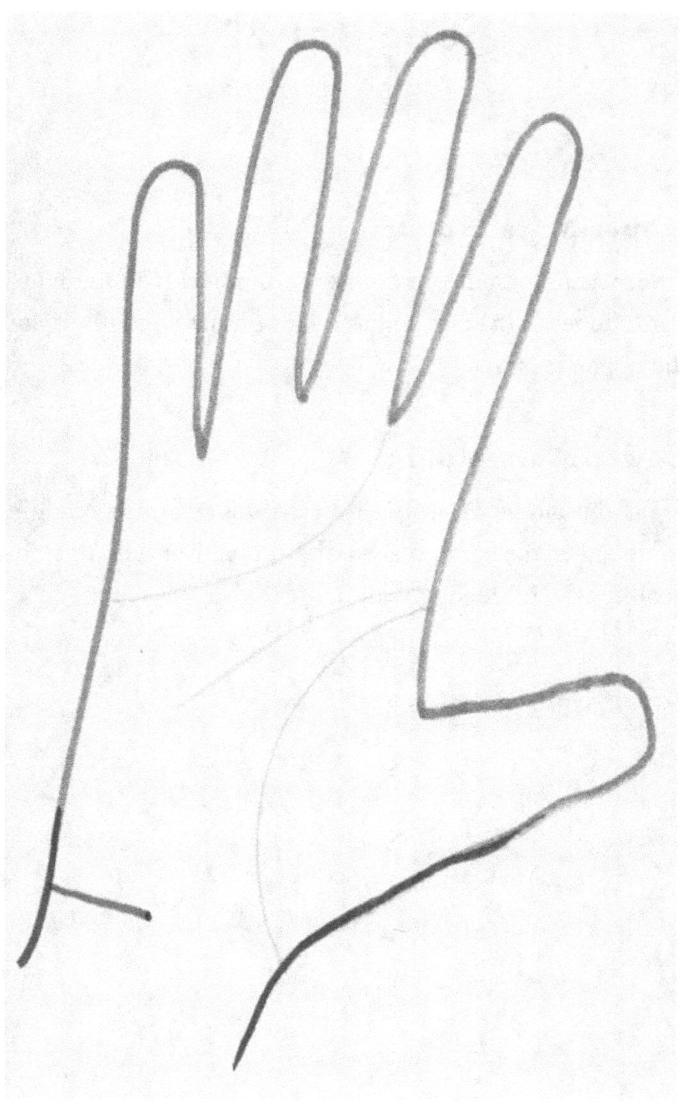

Chapter 22

Upper Mars Mount

Upper Mars mount represents the mother. If the mount is hard, it means the person has a lot of inner strength. If soft, the opposite is true.

Lower Mars Mount

If the mount is puffy, it means the person is retaining some anger for some reason and probably needs to find a healthy way of dealing with it.

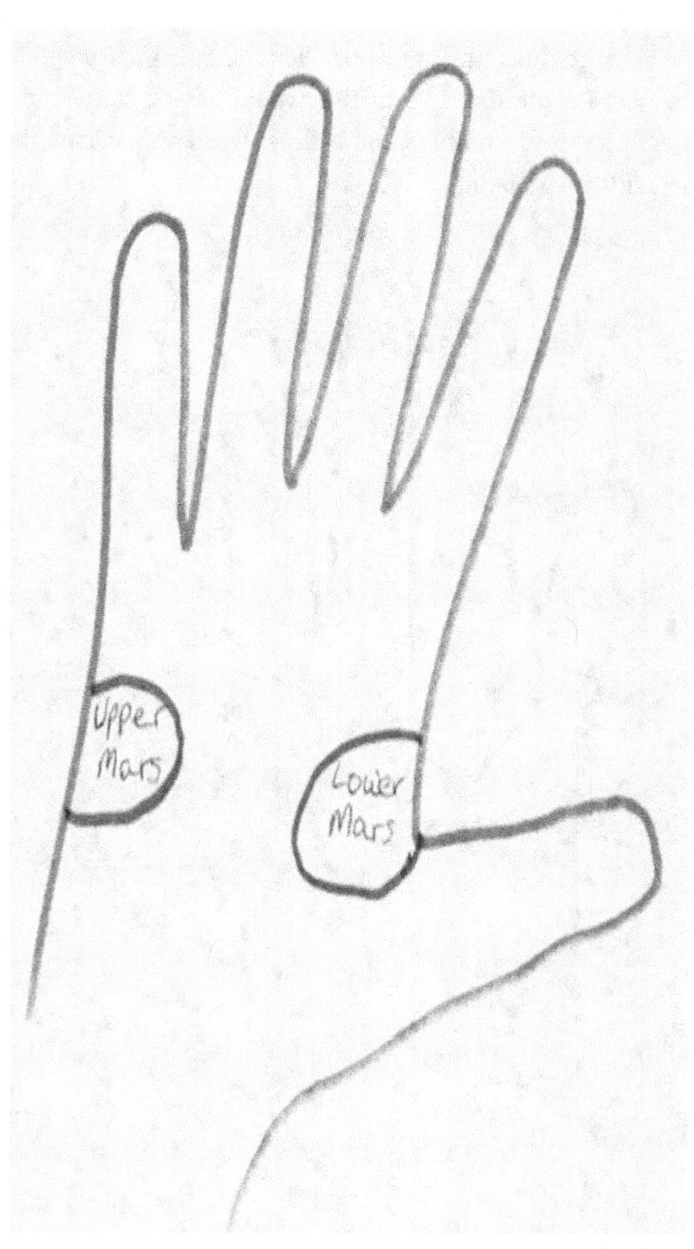

Upper Mars
Lower Mars

Luna

A large Luna mount means a love of the country and of the sea. People that like to fish would have a large Luna mount so would farmers and sailors. It also represents the person's imagination.

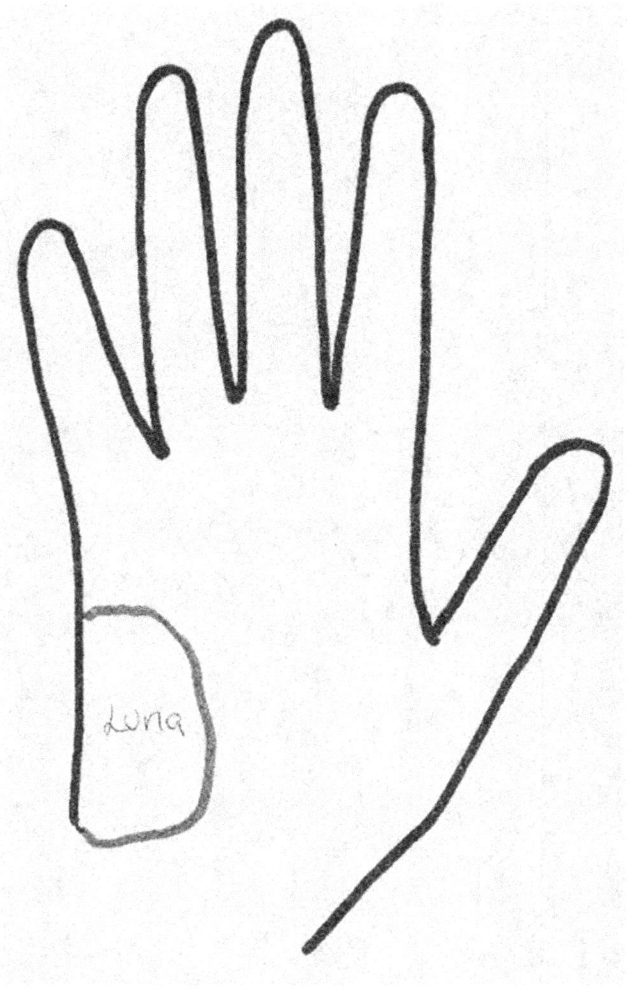

Neptune

Physically relates to women's things.

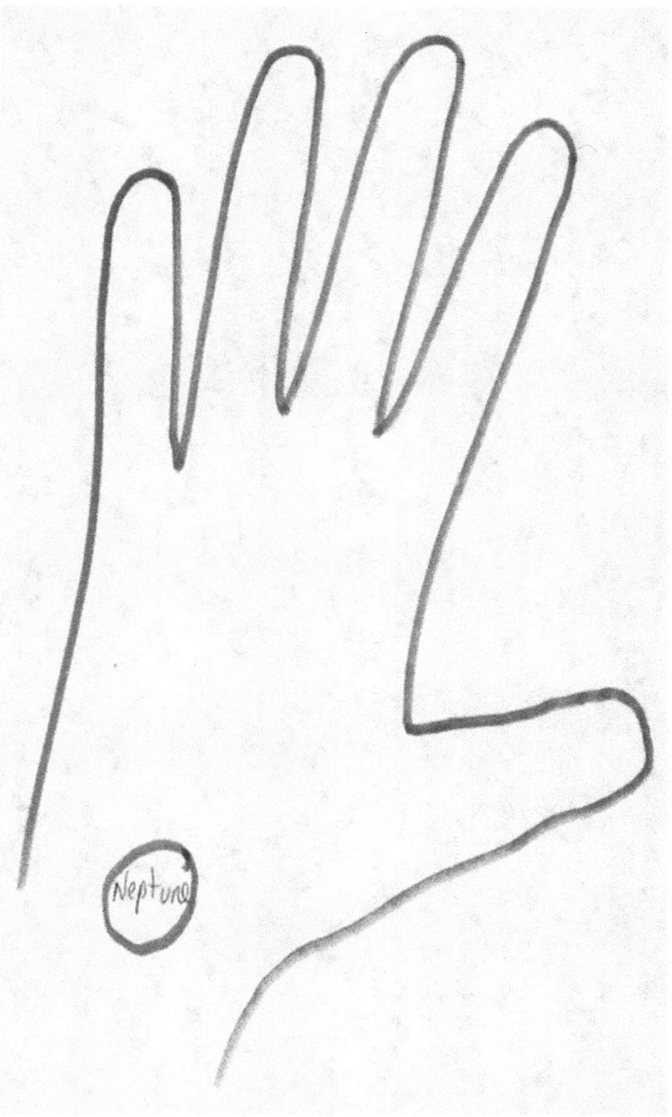

If the palm bows out from the Luna side of the hand

– The person will have some sort of talent.

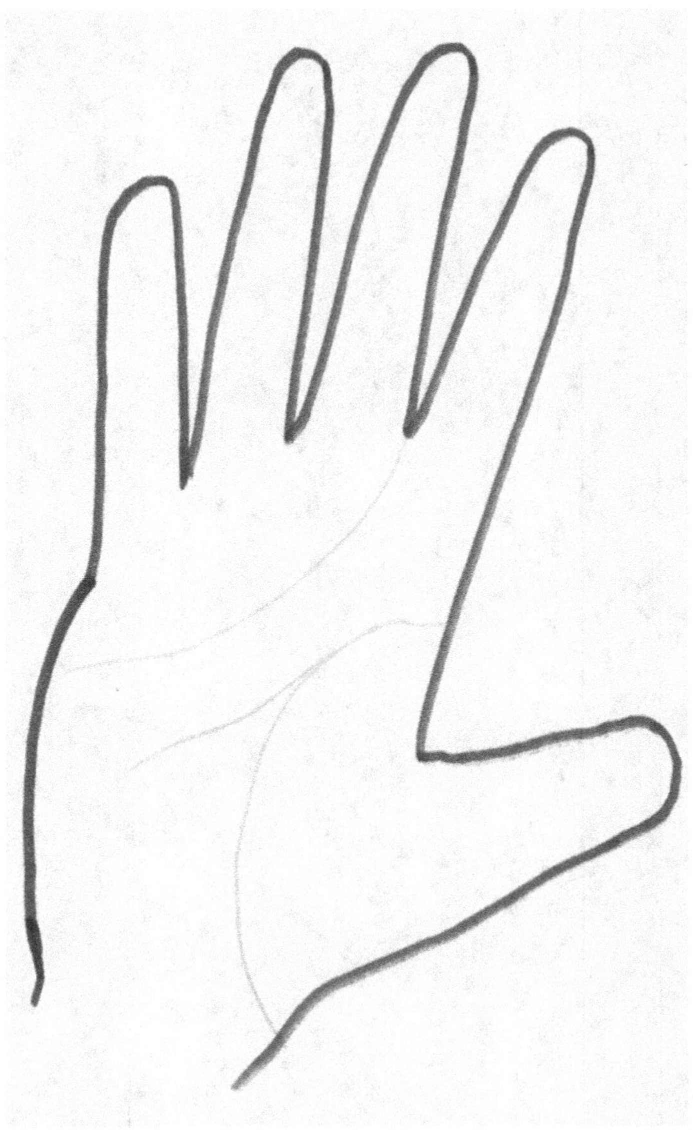

Chapter 23

Marriage Lines

Marriage lines are found on the Luna side of the hand, between the Heart line and the base of the little finger, but on the edge of the hand.

If it begins with a fork – Will know the person for quite some time before they got together.

If it does not have a fork at the beginning – It will be love at first sight. If the marriage line ends in a fork, it means divorce.

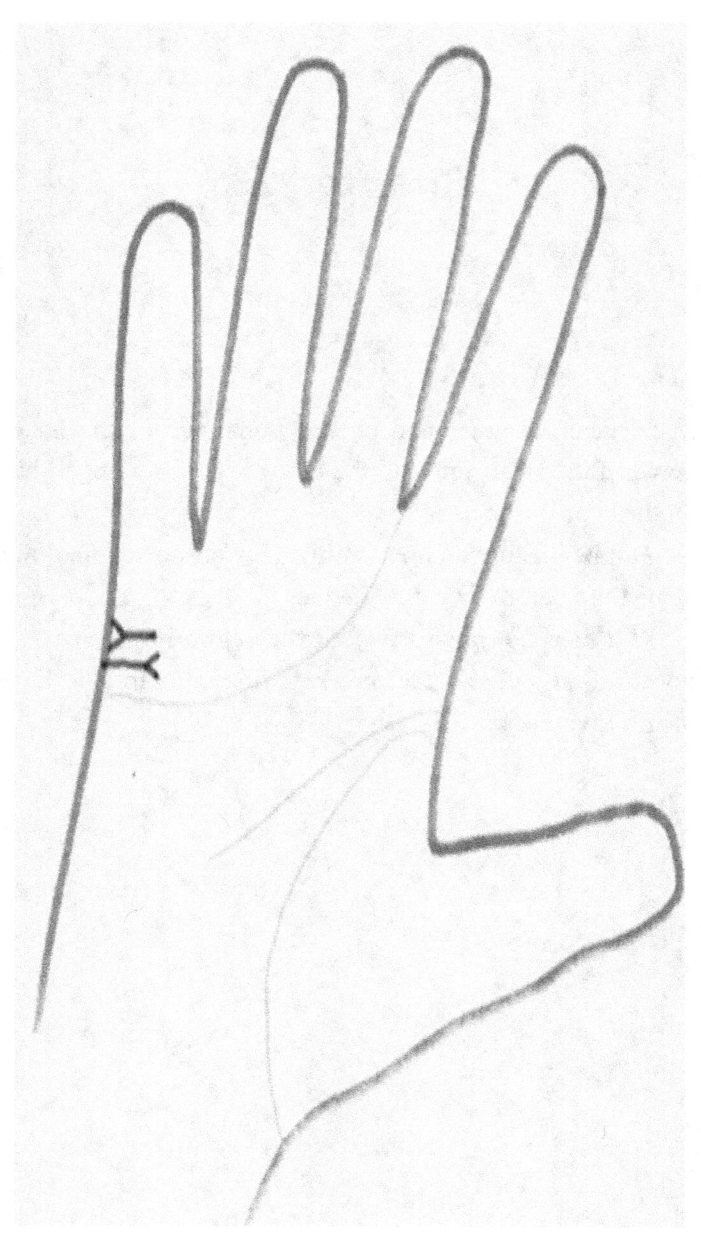

If it arcs down towards the mercury mount – It means the person is disappointed with the marriage and a health problem with their partner is shown.

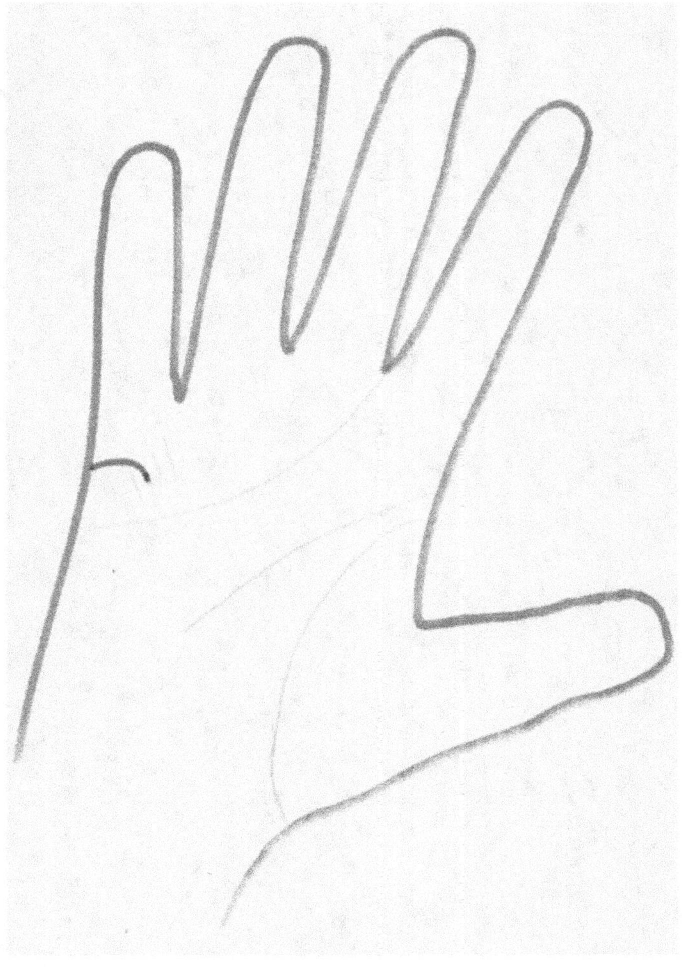

The deeper and longer the line, the deeper and longer the marriage will be.

The only time it does not mean a legal marriage – Is when there is a child connection; it will show up on the marriage lines.

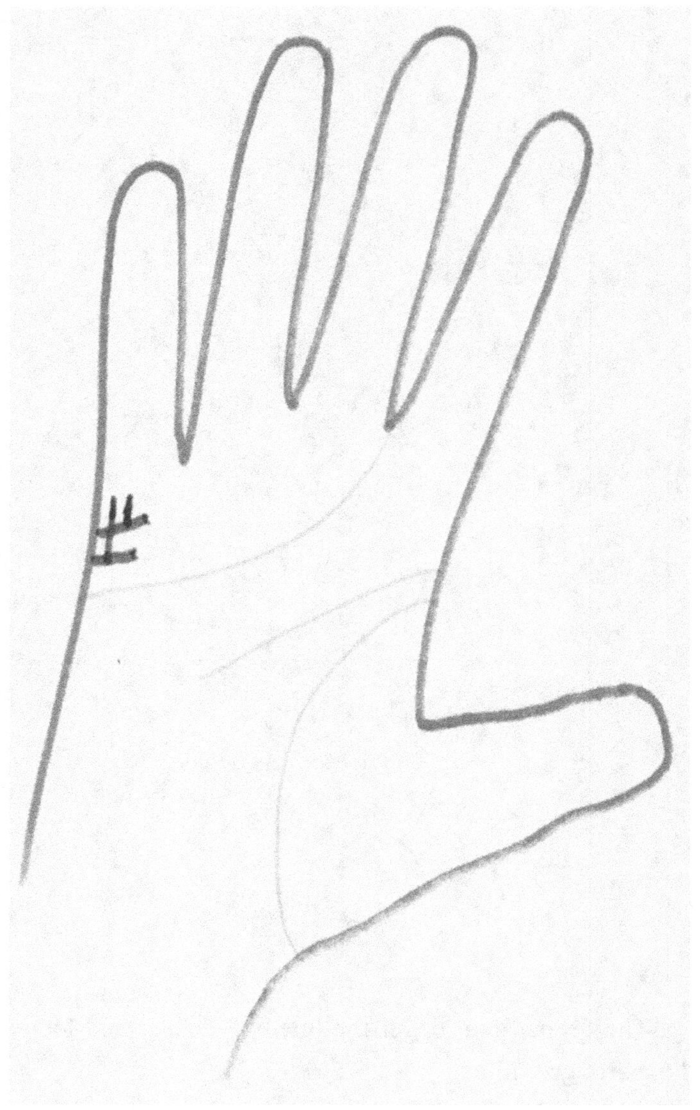

If there are parallel lines – In this area, it either means that the person's partner is having an affair or they are living separate lives.

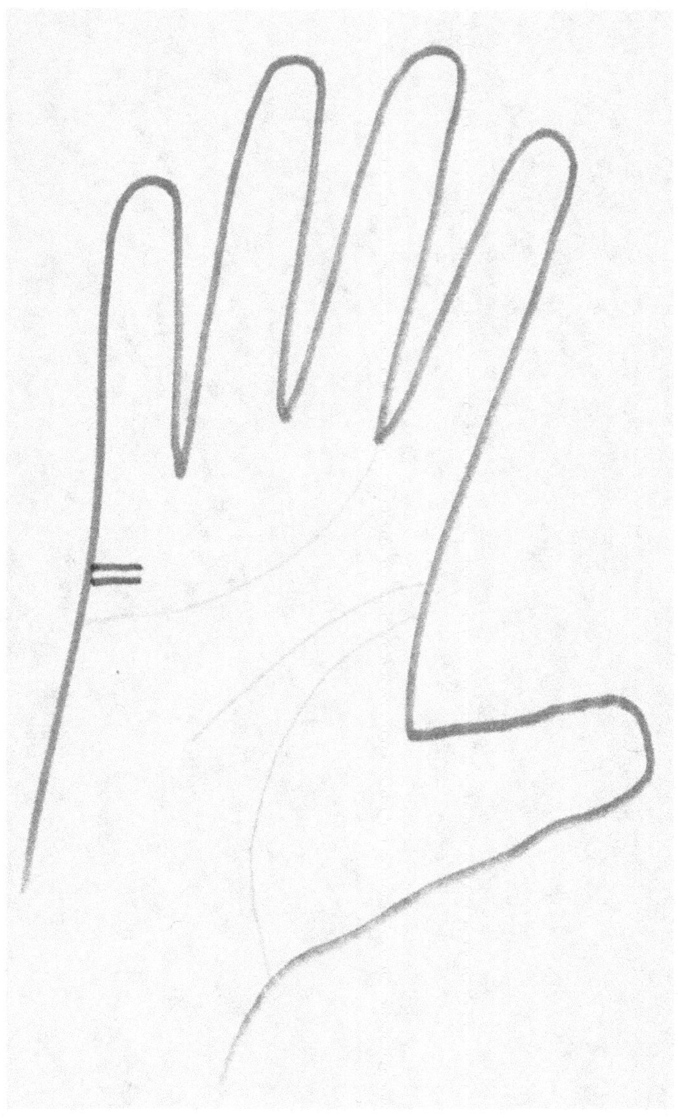

If there is a diagonal line rising from the marriage line – It means the person's partner will get a job or promotion at work.

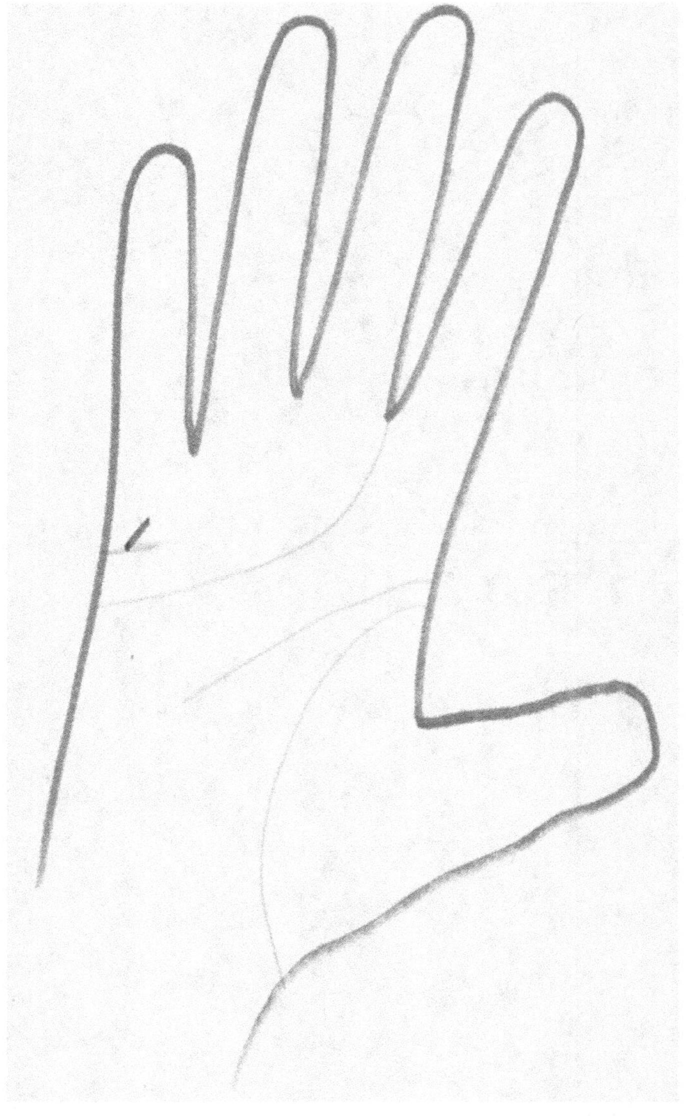

When the marriage line circles up and around the base of the Mercury finger – It means the death of their partner; it can appear three years before and at least three years after, if not more. If you do see this marking on a client's hand, start by attentively asking if their partner is still with us. If they say yes, just suggest they go to their doctor and get a checkup.

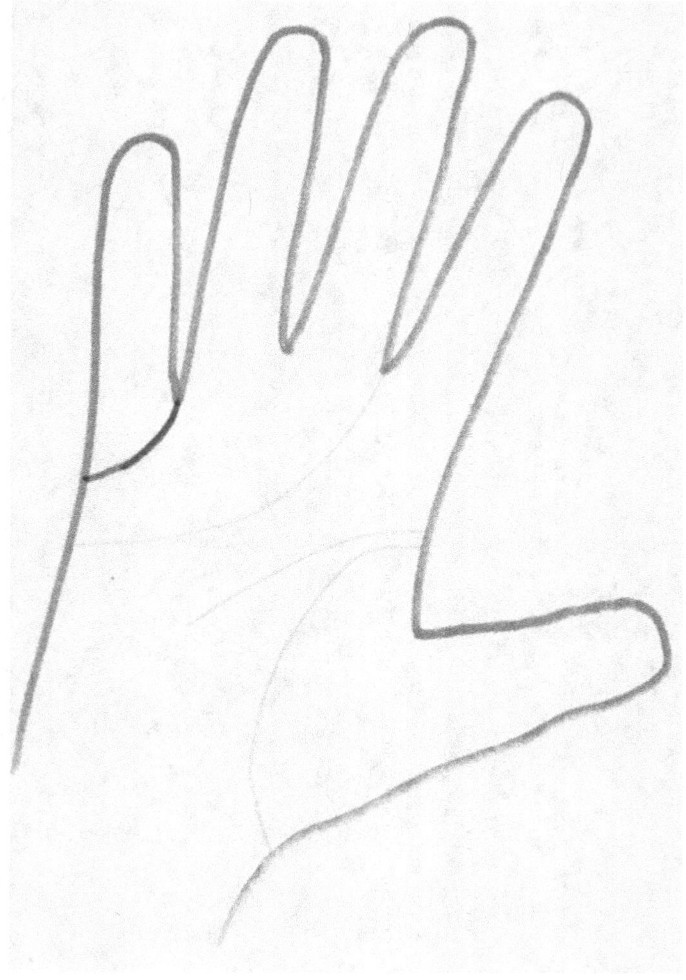

If the marriage line follows the heart line for a while
– It means the person likes to be in control, which can sometimes cause problems in their relationship and for the people around them.

Children

Children run vertically on the marriage lines. You used to be able to say the light ones are girls and the deeper ones are boys, but times have changed. Now we say that the light ones belong to children with a sensitive nature and the deeper one will belong to dominant-natured children. If you see a line which is not properly formed, it will be a miscarriage or an abortion.

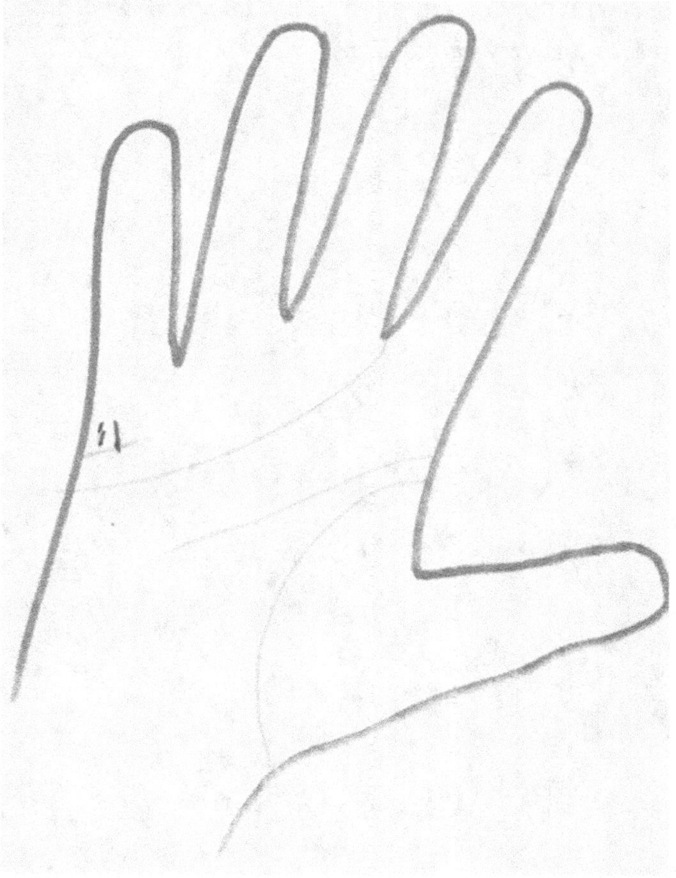

As people get older, their grandkids can start appearing on their hands also. If the person has a mother or father type of relationship with a child, they will appear as their kids on their hands, for example stepparents. Teachers will also have many child lines in this area, even if they have no children of their own. So, use your intuition as well as your knowledge. Even people's pets can appear as their kids in their hands. Sometimes, it helps to discuss what you are seeing to the client and it will make more sense to them.

You will definitely need to use talcum powder in this area, as it is very hard to see.

Chapter 24

Markings Found Anywhere on the Hand and What They Mean

A grill, like a tennis racket, means temporary depression in whichever part of the life where it is found on the hand. (a)

A square means protection. (b)

Triangles mean learning and education. (c)

A cross bar means an obstacle or represents an event in the person's life. (d)

A star with a tail means the death of a loved one. Where it is found on the hand is always meaningful. (e)

A diamond brings a feeling of being trapped for a certain amount of time, for example being hospitalized or jailed, or even a single parent may feel trapped in one area while the kids are in school.

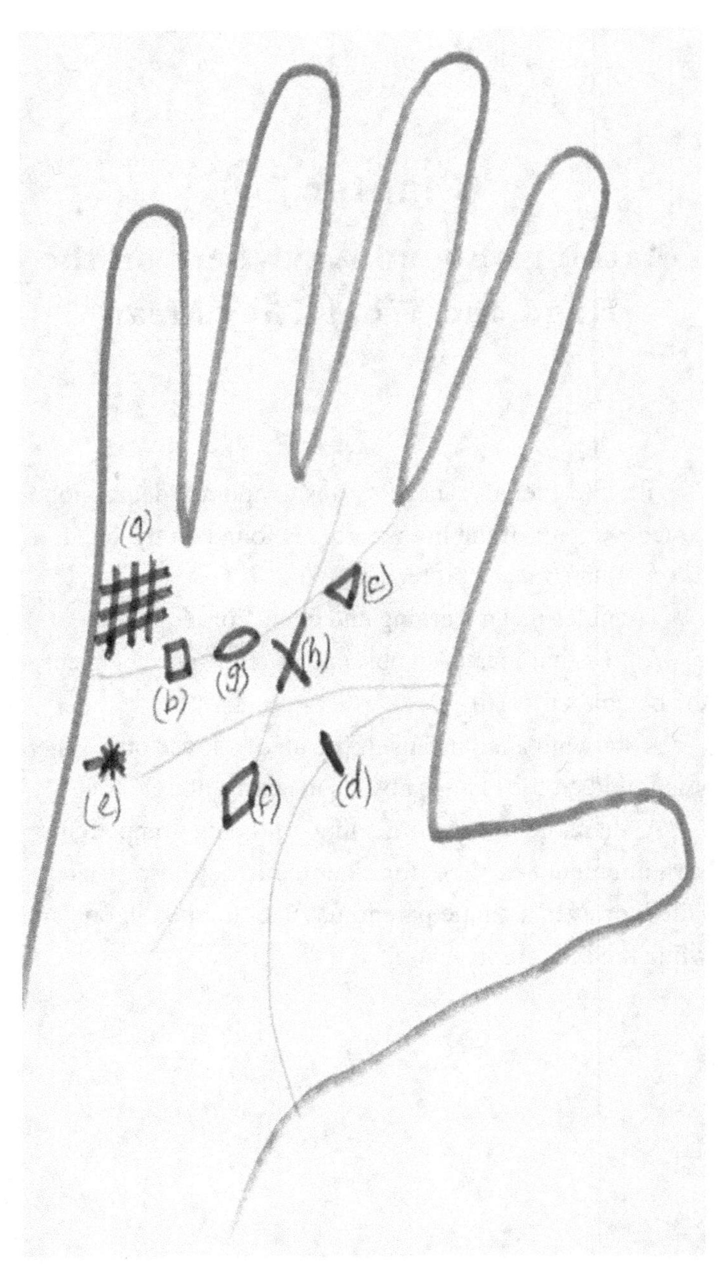

(a)
(b)
(c)
(d)
(e)
(f)
(g)
(h)

If there are a lot of lines on the hands, it means the person has a very busy mind and they can think on their feet, so to speak. They would probably benefit from doing some regular meditation, and not the usual kind, they have to do, what I call, open-eyed meditation, like admiring the view or even some fishing. When doing a reading, you don't have to read every single one of them, just the major ones. Every now and then, you will come across a person that has, what I call, worry lines. There are a lot of faint lines everywhere, which makes it hard to see the usual lines, but even harder to see the marriage and children lines. All you can do is just explain what you are seeing to the client.

If there are not many lines, it means the person knows how to switch off and zone out when they need to. It is definitely what I would class as a talent because a lot of people cannot do it.

Chapter 25
Full Dummy Readings

I will now do a couple of dummy readings.
Hands of a forty-two-year-old nurse.

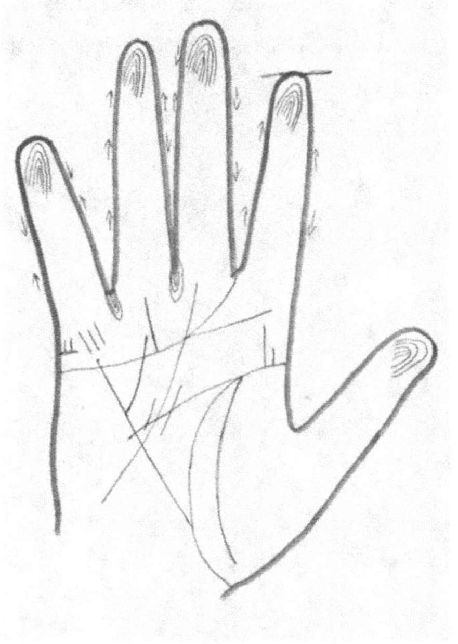

Left Hand

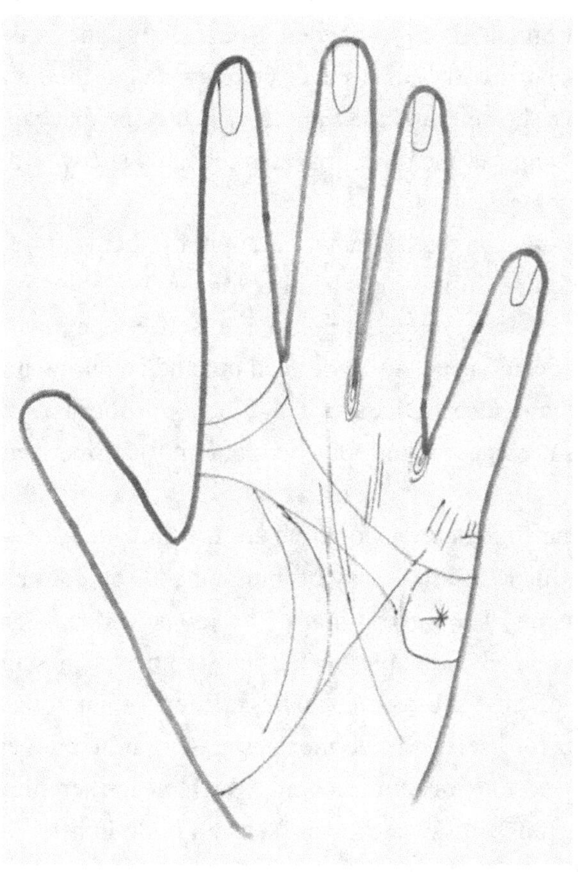

Right Hand

The palm is square and the fingers are the short, so they are earth hands. Which means the person is a hardworking, reliable, practical person, who prefers to concentrate on one activity at a time. She dislikes change and has a special connection to nature.

Having narrow nails, she will get the same effect just by admiring nature from the window, as she is more of an indoor person. After asking if she is right or left-handed, I found out she is right-handed. So, the left hand is the one she is born with and it never changes and is the hand she keeps to herself, and the right hand is the one that can grow and change as she does. It is also the hand she would show to the outside world.

I notice on the left hand: the Jupiter finger is quite short, but the one on the right hand is longer. Which shows that she has done some work on her self-esteem, which is fantastic and needs to be pointed out and congratulated.

I have also noticed that the veins on the back of her hands are not standing out, so she is not an over-sensitive person.

The fingers are smooth where the knuckles are, so she has a quick, intuitive way of thinking and she does not like arguments. The fingerprints are all loops, which means she is very much a people person and is good at making the most of any situation. She has a loop of humor, which speaks for itself and also means she is an animal lover. She also has a loop of serious intent, which means her intentions are serious with whatever she sets out to do in life.

She has a beautiful heart line, which means that she knows how to give and receive love and she also has a humanitarian streak as well.

She has worked hard from quite a young age and got help outside the family with that, shown by her fate (work) line starting on the Luna mount.

She also has a health striate, which means she would do well in the healing industry and has been working in the industry since the age of thirty-five, shown by the line coming from the health line up to the mount of Apollo.

She has also done a course of study and has always been good at making a dollar, shown by the strong money maker line.

During her late twenties and early thirties, she was busy doing three things such as work, motherhood, and study, shown by her fate lines.

The rings of Solomon show that she has a good understanding of people and can easily sympathize with them.

There is a star with a tail on the upper Mars mount, which is representative of the death of her mother having an impact on her. She also has a sister line on the inside of the life line, which kicks in at the age of nineteen, which is the age she was when her mother died, showing that she is now her daughter's guardian angel who protects her against accident and illness. Her mother died from dementia which also caused her daughter to have a freckle, which is an emotional blockage in that area of her life.

The hands also show that the lady is married to a man who she fell in love with at first sight and has two children as well.

From the age of forty onwards is when her happiness and success line started to kick in, so she will feel as if it was all worthwhile in the long run.

The next is a thirty-two-year-old tradesman.

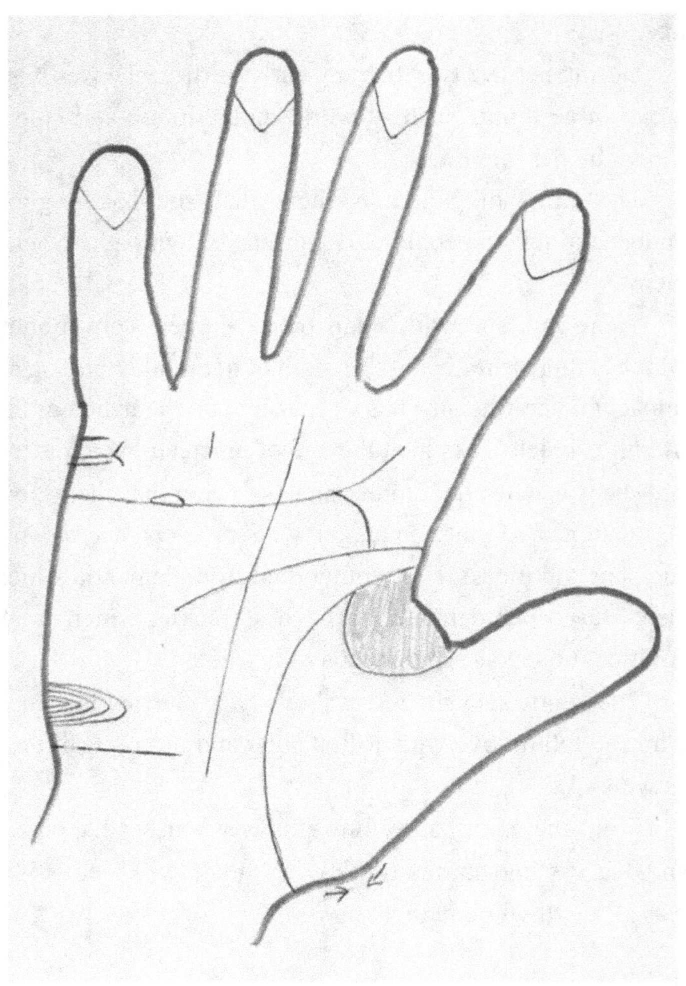

Left Hand

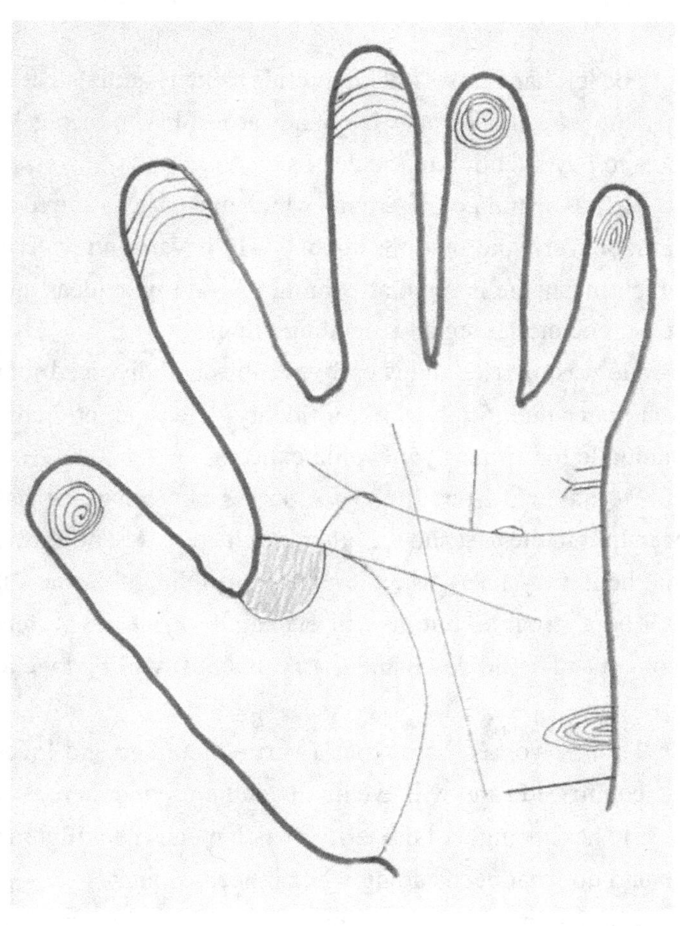

Right Hand

The palm is rectangular and the fingers are short, so these are fire hands. This person is always on the go and is very passionate about his work. He knows how to sway people and situations to go the way he wants.

Short fingers mean that he has a natural impatience to want things done yesterday. He has a wide palm, which means he likes his own space so he takes that when he needs to.

His left hand bows out on the side so he is quite talented in some way and because his hands are so big, it means he likes to pay attention to the details.

He has spatulate fingernails which means he is suited to outdoor work and outdoor hobbies. He is very innovative, which means he is good at coming up with new ideas and he is good at making and mending things.

He was married in his early twenties and divorced four years later due to his wife's infidelity. It was emotionally traumatic for him, as you would expect.

He has two heart lines, one shows how much he has been hurt in the past and the other is quite passive and shows that he is very fussy when it comes to finding a partner. It will be a struggle, but he will eventually meet the perfect woman and settle down and marry again. It will be love at first sight.

He has worked hard from a very young age and loves the countryside and will eventually end up living there.

He has an angle of dexterity, which means he will jump up and do what needs doing when it needs doing.

I notice that his Jupiter finger is jutting out to the side and is a little on the short side, which means he can be quite insecure in conjunction with a line of poison and a puffy lower Mars mount. This man has a problem with alcohol and tends to get loud and aggressive when he has too much to drink. This could be helped with a little professional guidance.

His fingerprints show a couple of different things. Firstly, his Jupiter finger, which is associated with his personal ambitions and goals, has an arch and so does his work finger, which makes him a very practical person who is very good with his hands in general. It also means he has a suspicious nature and needs proof; he needs to see to believe. He also prefers to control his emotions. When it comes to his creativity, he can be very intense according to the whorl print on his Apollo finger, which his thumb also has, which overrides the others at times. He is definitely a one of a kind.

I notice, he does not have too many lines on his hands, so he has a natural ability to switch off and zone out when he needs to.

I also notice that his Mercury fingers are crooked, which means he keeps a certain part of himself hidden from the outside world and he also knows how to bend the truth a bit when he wants to.

Due to his unbending thumbs, he can be quite stubborn and would suit a lady who has flexible thumbs. He is also ruled by his head and has always had a lot of will power and determination, shown by the padding on the top of his thumbs.

He is also getting better with his budget as he is getting older, shown by the difference in the gaps between the Saturn and Apollo fingers on both hands.

I also notice the gap between Jupiter and his thumb is wider on the left hand, which means when he was younger, he was quite open and generous in nature and as he is getting older, the right one shows that he is starting to get a little shy and self-protective.

In Conclusion

Palmistry is not only a tool for others but also to get to know yourself better, as in your strengths, talents, and also your weaknesses, so you know how to deal with yourself when you have to and make improvements and precautions where necessary. You can do a 15-minute reading on a person and you will know them better than they will ever know themselves over their whole lifetime and how they can improve on anything that will make their lives easier and more fulfilling – all the more reason to record their reading for them, so they have it to look back on when they feel the need.